GRAND PRÉ

LANDSCAPE FOR THE WORLD

A. J. B. Johnston and Ronnie-Gilles LeBlanc

NIMBUS
PUBLISHING LTD

For Parker and Bayly
–AJB JOHNSTON

For Rachel
–RONNIE-GILLES LEBLANC

Nimbus Publishing Limited
3731 Mackintosh St, Halifax, NS B3K 5A5
(902) 455-4286 nimbus.ca

Printed and bound in Canada

NB1099

Design: Jenn Embree

Cover photo: © Jamie Robertson

Library and Archives Canada Cataloguing in Publication

Johnston, A. J. B., author
Grand Pré : landscape for the world / A. J. B. Johnston and Ronnie-Gilles LeBlanc.
(Stories of our past)
    Includes bibliographical references.
    ISBN 978-1-77108-271-6 (pbk.)

1. Grand Pré (N.S.)—History. I. LeBlanc, Ronnie Gilles, 1952-, author II. Title.
III. Series: Stories of our past (Halifax, N.S.)

FC2314.G72J65 2015   971.6'34   C2014-907764-5

 Canada Council   Conseil des arts
for the Arts   du Canada

Nimbus Publishing acknowledges the financial support for its publishing activities from the Government of Canada through the Canada Book Fund (CBF) and the Canada Council for the Arts, and from the Province of Nova Scotia through Film & Creative Industries Nova Scotia. We are pleased to work in partnership with Film & Creative Industries Nova Scotia to develop and promote our creative industries for the benefit of all Nova Scotians.

CONTENTS

Introduction   1

Chapter 1:   Layers and Lenses   5
Chapter 2:   Long, Long Ago   13
Chapter 3:   First Peoples   23
Chapter 4:   The Acadian Era   37
Chapter 5:   Times of Trouble   59
Chapter 6:   The Coming of the New England Planters   81
Chapter 7:   Memory and Recognition   97

Acknowledgements   115
Bibliography   116
Image Credits   119
Index   120

Few of us are lucky enough to see the Landscape of Grand Pré World Heritage Site from a low-flying plane. Mark Eastman took this photo as the plane approached Long Island, coming in from the Minas Basin. In the distance, on the other side of the patchwork quilt of fields, lies the village of Grand Pré on the gently rising ground.

INTRODUCTION

GREAT THINGS OFTEN BEGIN in small ways; they are equally the fruit of time and commitment. When Acadian scholars, alarmed with the way Grand-Pré National Historic Site had declined, met with Parks Canada officials in 1982 to assert the site's importance and the need to care for it properly, no one in the room foresaw that the most cherished of all Acadian places would, thirty years later, be at the heart of a UNESCO World Heritage Site. Yet that is how the path towards international recognition began: with people deeply motivated by a sense of history, passion, and community, who played their part in a long sequence of events necessary to keep a memory alive.

Of course, as this book by John and Ronnie-Gilles demonstrates, the story of Grand Pré stretches back much farther than 1982. It is a tale with a cast of thousands, each member carrying the legacy of his community's values: Mi'kmaq, Acadian, New England Planter, Loyalist, Dutch, and others. Certain individuals stand out for the roles they played in making Grand Pré noteworthy in humanity's history—Henry Wadsworth Longfellow, John Frederic Herbin, and Pascal Poirier to name a few—but they were instruments of peoples' voices, stories, and aspirations.

Little would have been accomplished on this project of recognition without lasting relationships developed and maintained over the years. Accordingly, we thank the Mi'kmaw, Acadian, Grand Pré and area communities; the Grand Pré

THE LANDSCAPE OF GRAND PRÉ |
LE PAYSAGE DE GRAND-PRÉ (NS)

CANADA 1.20

Canada Post selected essentially the same iconic shot for its commemorative stamp of Grand Pré as we did for the cover of this book. Countless amateur photographers take the same photo and will continue to do so for years to come.

Marsh Body; the universities of Acadia, Saint Mary's, Moncton, and Sainte-Anne; and government organizations: Parks Canada, the Municipality of the County of Kings, the Province of Nova Scotia, the Atlantic Canada Opportunities Agency, and the former Kings Regional Development Authority. To show their ongoing commitment, most of these groups contribute to the work of the Landscape of Grand Pré Society, a not-for-profit organization whose mandate is to ensure the conservation, protection, presentation, and transmission to future generations of the property's Outstanding Universal Value.

The efforts and hopes of all who had toiled over the centuries to make Grand Pré and area their home, a vibrant agricultural community, and a powerful place of memory, resonated with many when, on June 30, 2012, UNESCO's World Heritage Committee declared at its meeting in St. Petersburg, Russia, that the Landscape of Grand Pré had become part of the "world heritage of mankind as a whole." What an emotionally charged moment to experience for all involved, knowing that each played a part in making history, partaking in 250 years of agricultural livelihood, struggle, peace, and reconciliation. The five years of preparing plans and documents to submit to UNESCO were the easy part. It is the centuries of layered accomplishments and tragedies, not to mention the labour and memories of all the peoples connected to this land, that give meaning to Grand Pré. Those people, past and present, created the landscape and made it thrive; many voices from different backgrounds, with a common bond to the exceptional Landscape of Grand Pré.

–Claude DeGrâce, Co-Chair, Landscape of Grand Pré Society, and Christophe Rivet, PhD, Project Manager, Nomination Grand Pré

This composite aerial photo presents the entirety of the Landscape of Grand Pré World Heritage Site and most of the buffer zone as well.

CHAPTER 1

LAYERS AND LENSES

In the Acadian land, on the shore of the Basin of Minas,
Distant, secluded, still, the little village of Grand-Pré
Lay in the fruitful valley. Vast meadows stretched to the eastward,
Giving the village its name...

–EVANGELINE, A TALE OF ACADIE,
HENRY WADSWORTH LONGFELLOW, 1847

GRAND PRÉ: ONLY TWO words, yet what evocative power they possess. For Grand Pré is not just a village on the map of Kings County, Nova Scotia, but a name bestowed with multiple layers of history and meaning, which radiate across Canada and around the world.

The Grand Pré that greets a first glance is an unassuming, charming place: leafy trees, orchards, vineyards, farmland, a few dozen houses and barns. It's when you know the area's history, however, that the picturesque acquires deep import. For there's the Grand Pré that originally was, the one it became, and those that developed after that. Intriguingly, they are all linked. And those eras have more in common than not. Across a span of more than

This turn-of-the-twentieth-century photo depicts the village of Grand Pré on either side of the Old Post Road, which is thought to date back to Acadian times. Many buildings shown here are still standing.

Which Grand Pré is That?

We apologize, but what we mean by Grand Pré in this book might vary from time to time. Rarely will it be limited to mean exclusively today's village community of that name. Our Grand Pré is closer to late seventeenth- and early eighteenth-century usage. In other words, when we write "Grand Pré" we are usually referring to its UNESCO World Heritage Site boundaries. The WHS includes all of the Grand Pré Marsh and portions of the separate communities of North Grand Pré, Hortonville, Grand Pré, and Lower Wolfville.

three hundred years—mostly in peace but occasionally in times of war—Grand Pré helped shape Canada's history and character.

In the summer of 2012 the "Landscape of Grand Pré" was proclaimed a UNESCO (United Nations Educational, Scientific and Cultural Organization) World Heritage Site, the third in Nova Scotia and sixteenth in Canada. Now, especially since the

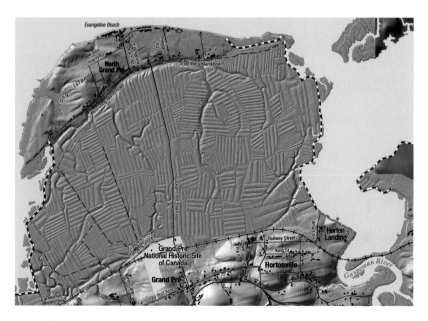

A LiDAR image of the Landscape of Grand Pré WHS, identified by the dotted red line, which reveals the landform beneath the grass and trees.

designation, this area of simple, rural beauty is recognized as standing for values that are universally admired.

Grand Pré is, undoubtedly, most commonly associated with the Acadian people and their traumatic history. Though the Acadians reclaimed salt marshes and lived in many locations throughout the Maritimes well before their forced removal (1755–62), it is Grand Pré that is most closely associated with what the Acadians call the Grand Dérangement. Since the nineteenth century, the village of Grand Pré, a few kilometres from Wolfville, has been the symbolic agricultural homeland of what the Acadian people once possessed, and which was abruptly taken away.

American poet Henry Wadsworth Longfellow first linked the tragedy known as the Acadian Deportation to Grand Pré in 1847, and that link only grew in the years that followed. In the twentieth century, it would be at Grand Pré that Acadians (and non-Acadians, it must be said) erected poignant memorials to what had happened in 1755, making the area the most evocative and

The statue of Evangeline, with the Memorial Church in the background.

powerful of the many Acadian history sites. The French term for these places is *lieu de mémoire*, which, in the case of Grand Pré, tends to be said reverentially.

Yet the touching lens of Acadian memory and loss is only one layer of Grand Pré. A quite different lens focuses on the area's remarkable engineering accomplishments. In the face of the highest tides in the world, the original Acadian farm community, using only simple tools and great ingenuity, succeeded in adapting a European technology to claim a vast wetland from the sea. Their newly created dykelands would become some of the most productive agricultural land at that latitude in North America.

Of course, creating something wonderful is only ever the beginning of any story; wonderful things must also be maintained. And for that part of the Grand Pré story, we shift from the Acadians and acknowledge those who came after the 1755 Deportation to take over the Acadian lands—not only at Grand Pré but in many other locations as well—who kept the fertile dykelands protected from the Minas Basin.

The first wave of non-Acadian settlers to the Grand Pré area are known to history as the New England Planters. ("Planter" was a seventeenth- and eighteenth-century term for settler.) Invited by the British colonial administration of Nova Scotia to take over the post-Deportation Acadian lands, the New England Planters were able to repair, maintain, and eventually expand on what the Acadians had done at Grand Pré. This was a remarkable feat, and a subject we discuss further in chapter 6. The point to retain right now is that the dykes protecting the Grand Pré Marsh are not something that can be forgotten about. As long as the highly fertile dykeland lies below

Dykeland = Polder

In much of the rest of the world, the term for such land claimed from the sea is the Dutch word "polder." Throughout this book, however, we follow the Kings County usage and employ the words "dykeland" and "marsh" where "polder" would be the internationally recognized term.

Dyke or dike?

In English, there are two ways to spell the word for this type of raised earthen embankment. The authors of this book have chosen the "y" version, but to spell it with an "i" is also correct. It depends on the dictionary one consults. In some parts of the world the term would be "levee." Another confusing element is that the word "dyke" is also used in the Grand Pré area and elsewhere in the Annapolis Valley to mean not only the embankment but also the arable land protected behind the raised earthen walls (i.e., the dykeland).

the high-water mark, which it does, someone must continue looking after the dykes on a regular basis. In recent years, this has been the responsibility of the Nova Scotia Department of Agriculture. Like the Acadians and the Planters, today's technical specialists must keep an eye on—and occasionally repair or top up—the dykes to ensure that the legacy of the fertile landscape at Grand Pré endures.

There is yet another layer of meaning attached to Grand Pré. Some might say it's an aura. It builds on the associations people bring with them when they visit the area. For some, this familiarity of place began with a history book, a poem, or a song—or maybe a novel, a film, or a piece of art. Whatever the source, the name "Grand Pré" conjures up an imaginary world, one created by the artists who were inspired by the area. Of the many personages who inhabit such creations, it is un-questionably Longfellow's Evangeline who domi-nates the associative landscape of Grand Pré.

There are today five aboiteaux in place to drain the Grand Pré Marsh. Though made of modern materials, they function in ex-actly the same way as the original Acadian sluices made of hollowed logs or constructed as boxes.

Today's farmers use modern equipment on the centuries-old dykeland.

Still another way of looking at Grand Pré is through the lens of commemoration. It turns out there are two Canadian national historic sites called Grand Pré. One has a hyphen (Grand-Pré) and the other does not. The former is administered by Parks Canada and emphasizes the Acadian storylines between the years 1680 and 1755 as well as the Acadians' later symbolic return to erect evocative monuments. The latter is much larger and celebrates the multi-layered rural landscape that makes up the overall area, from the Gaspereau River, up over the ridge and down, to include Long Island/North Grand Pré. And now there is a third commemoration, with another set of boundaries, that of Grand Pré as a UNESCO World Heritage Site. Amplifying those honours, the 1747 Attack

Across the Span of Time

The continuity of agriculture at Grand Pré across more than three centuries is worth reflecting upon. What the Acadians began, the New England Planters continued. Today the same landscape is a source of livelihood to the area's farmers, some of which descend from Planters and many who do not. Regardless of any Grand Pré resident's particular family tree, the human attachment to the landscape of Grand Pré is as strong among today's residents as it was back in Acadian and Planter times. And across that span of time, the people of Grand Pré have chosen to live on the upland, while farming the dykeland below.

at Grand Pré is an event of national significance, former prime minister Robert Laird Borden is a person of national significance, and the nearby Covenanters' Church is a site of national significance. There surely cannot be many places in the world with such an abundance of official designations in a small area.

Artists of all ages and genres find inspiration in Grand Pré.

For a century and a half after the Acadian Deportation, Grand Pré was known by a different name: Horton Township, a name given by the New England Planters after they arrived in 1760. The vast dykeland, however, the Planters left unchanged. They called it Grand Pré Marsh, the name it still has. "Horton Township" would endure until late in the nineteenth century, when the descendants of the Planters (as well as others who had moved to the area) revived the original Acadian name for the village, Grand Pré. Today, the Horton name lives on at adjacent Hortonville and nearby Horton Landing.

In the language of historians and geographers, Grand Pré is what's known as a cultural landscape. That is, it is not a terrain created strictly by nature, but one that shows the impact of highly significant human interventions. Some of those interventions—the dykeland, property lines, and roads—have been in place since the late seventeenth and early eighteenth centuries. Other elements—the Memorial Church, Evangeline Statue, Herbin Cross, and Deportation Cross—were introduced in the twentieth century. Together, they create a corner of the world that is subtle and deep, poignant and rich.

The mud flats along the Minas Basin are vast.

CHAPTER 2

LONG, LONG AGO

O marshes green, the dykes of Acadie,
I have been nursed upon your ancient breast.

–J. F. HERBIN, 1909

THE NATURAL SETTING AT Grand Pré is exceptional, and not just because it's picturesque. It's also fascinating from both a natural and an historical point of view. Grand Pré did not just happen to become a great place for agriculture with a rich history. What happened there did so precisely because of the fertile interrelationship of the land and sea in the area. The

At high tide the swirling water of the Minas Basin churns away at the sandstone cliffs along the shoreline, giving the muddy waters their distinctive hue.

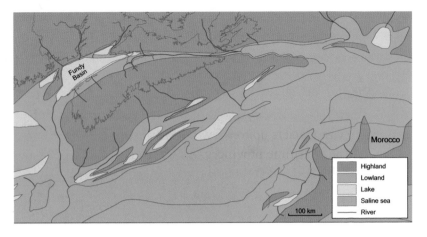

This map depicts the geography of parts of present-day Atlantic Canada and adjacent northwestern Africa 203 million years ago, during the Late Triassic period and just prior to outpourings of lava familiar today around Fundy shores as the North Mountain Basalt.

remarkable productivity of Grand Pré's dykeland arises from conditions caused by natural processes in the Minas Basin. The human element came later on, and when it did, it effected changes that generated three and a quarter centuries of highly productive agriculture, which continues today. Our story of the Landscape of Grand Pré begins a long time ago.

THE CREATION OF AN ESTUARINE ENVIRONMENT

We could begin our history two hundred million years ago, when the Minas Basin was a dry land-rift valley located on a tectonic plate situated somewhere near the equator. If that's too far back, we could jump a hundred million years and find the rift valley (today's water-filled Minas Basin) on its plate moving at a continental-drift pace—a few centimetres a year—at a higher latitude. Somewhere about halfway between the equator and the North Pole, that plate collided with another, as all plates eventually do. One consequence of this collision was a new landform, which people in Nova Scotia recognize as their home province. In the vocabulary of commerce, you could consider this ancient collision an early merger or acquisition.

We now jump ahead millions of years to the end of the last ice age, when vast glaciers up to a few kilometres thick covered virtually all of the Maritime provinces. As these glaciers began to melt and retreat about fourteen thousand years ago, sea levels around the planet started to rise. (This will sound familiar to anyone paying attention to climate change, but that's another story.) The Bay of Fundy became ice free before the land. As the glaciers retreated northward, the underlying seabed began to rebound with the weight of the ice removed. For every kilometre of ice thickness, the land mass beneath was pushed down three hundred metres.

The global warming that began roughly 14,000 years BP (Before Present) did not, however, follow a constant warming pattern. Maybe thirty centuries in, about 11,000 years BP, there was a reversal, including a temperature decline that some scientists speculate was caused by a meteorite exploding above North America. Whatever the cause, global temperatures dropped an average of seven to eight degrees, with the drop even more pronounced in Atlantic Canada. Human habitation in the Maritimes would have been difficult to say the least. The extended cold period, called the Younger Dryas, lasted about 1,300 years and brought about a return to nearly full glaciation and the spread of tundra-like conditions. It is one that has a bearing on our story of the Landscape of Grand Pré and the adjacent Minas Basin.

During the warming periods before and after the Younger Dryas, rivers from the melting ice sheets washed huge quantities of soil into the sea. The bottom of what we now call the Bay of Fundy became covered in sediment. When exactly an early version of the Minas Basin came into existence is not easy to say. At times seawater could be found in the lowest-lying parts of what is now

What is the Younger Dryas?

The word "*dryas*" refers to a plant in the rose family, which is widely distributed in the northern portions of Eurasia and North America where there is tundra. During glacial or near-glacial eras, such plants were found in much lower latitudes, as can be determined today by pollen analysis. Scientists identify three separate cold climatic phases they call Dryas. The one we are interested in, the Younger Dryas, is dated to circa 11,000–10,000 BP.

the basin (former rift valley) but not to any great depth. After the retreat of the glaciers, the rise of the seabed meant the basin was shallow at best. Afterwards, the return to near-glacial conditions during the Younger Dryas caused sea level to drop once again, as the water turned back into ice. Thus, the Minas Basin we know today is a relatively recent development, geologically speaking.

Nothing makes that fact more apparent than what we find if we explore what's out there. People who follow the tide charts can, with the right footwear, make their way at low tide far out into the Minas Basin near Grand Pré. There, they will find the stumps of ancient trees that, several thousand years ago, were growing on dry land. Now the stumps are located under the sea twice each day. It can be scary or exciting, depending on your point of view.

Difficult as it might be to imagine, as of twelve thousand years ago, the ocean had not yet risen enough to form the Northumberland Strait; what we think of as Prince Edward Island was still joined to the mainland of Canada; Georges and Browns Banks, now well offshore, were dry land; and Halifax's inner harbour, the Bedford Basin, was a lake. Eventually, as melting continued and the sea level rose, the landscape and seascape as we know it today gradually took shape. One of the last holdouts against the rising seawater of Atlantic Canada was the Minas Basin. Recall that if the water were removed it would be an arrowhead-shaped rift valley left behind from a long-ago collision of two continental plates.

After the Younger Dryas ended and the climate began to warm again, about 10,000 years BP, the ice vanished and sea level began to rise, as it continues to do today. Seawater, however, was prevented from entering the Minas Basin in its entirety. There was a huge gravel barrier stretching from Cape Blomidon to what we know today as the Parrsboro shore. There was only a narrow tidal channel connecting the valley's shallow lake to the Bay of Fundy.

As we know, there is no gravel barrier across the basin today. A team of ocean scientists, including John Shaw of the Geological Survey of Canada, concluded that the breakthrough in the gravel barrier occurred between 3,000 and 4,000 years BP—practically yesterday, in geological time—causing a flood tide of seawater from the Bay of Fundy into the valley, which connected the two, and creating the water body called the Minas Basin. Remarkably, at least one Mi'kmaw legend relates this geological event. We say more about that legend in the next chapter.

Once the Minas Basin became a triangular offshoot of the Bay of Fundy, it became a marine environment and began to feel the effects of ocean tides. Initially—meaning about 3,500 years BP—the tidal range in the Minas Basin was only about 1 to 1.5 metres, a far cry from what it is today. Those ranges increased dramatically over the centuries as

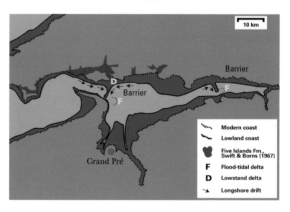

In geological terms, the shoreline of the Minas Basin that we know today—shown in green—only took its current form recently. For most of the early Holocene period, until 3,000 to 4,000 years BP, there was a delta (and barrier) across its narrowest point. This feature kept seawater from extending as far inland as it does today.

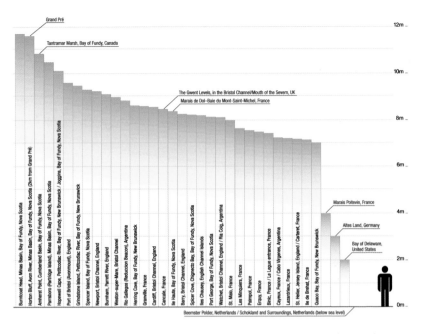

The exceptional setting along the Minas Basin and at Grand Pré is demonstrated on this graph; it illustrates the mean tidal ranges of locations capable of supporting agriculture among the top fifty highest tides in the world. Several of these locations are World Heritage Sites. In the UNESCO evaluation process, the Landscape of Grand Pré was compared to some of these places to make sure that it was indeed exceptional and possessing of outstanding universal value.

the worldwide sea level continued to rise. Today the average tidal range in the Minas Basin is about 12 metres, with spring tides occasionally reaching 16 metres, making them the highest recorded tides in the world. With storms and accompanying sea surges, the high tides can go higher still, overcoming dykes and causing devastation.

So what, you might ask, if the tides of the Minas Basin are the highest recorded in the world? At first, it may not seem like much of a claim. Yet it is. The tidal ranges within the Bay of Fundy in

This is a photo of a section of a natural salt marsh outside the enclosed dyke-land at Grand Pré. Before the Acadians arrived and began their massive reclamation work, what is now the farmable dry land of the Grand Pré Marsh would have looked like this.

Here is another stretch of natural salt marsh beyond the dyke. Please note the different grasses: in the foreground is *Juncus gerardii*, known as salt-marsh rush; farther back, closer to the water of the Gaspereau River, is *Spartina patens*, or marsh hay. These two naturally growing marsh grasses played important roles in the story of the Landscape of Grand Pré.

general and the Minas Basin in particular are forces to be reckoned with. On the Northumberland Strait between Prince Edward Island, Nova Scotia, and New Brunswick, the average tidal range is 1.2 metres. Along the South Shore of Nova Scotia, tidal heights typically vary between 2 and 2.6 metres. Near Yarmouth they rise to a little over 4 metres, while at the mouth of the Annapolis Basin, within which Acadians began their dyking projects in the 1630s, daily tidal ranges can reach up to about 8.5 metres. These

100 Billion Tonnes

Today, twice daily as part of the tidal cycle, 100 billion tonnes of seawater flow in and out of the Bay of Fundy. That's more water than the combined flow of all the world's rivers. The largest area covered by water is quite shallow. The central parts of the Minas Basin are only 25 to 30 metres deep at low tide. Yet the vertical aspect is only half the story. In some areas, the horizontal distance between high- and low-water lines is 5 kilometres. Because the water is so shallow, it creates an enormous intertidal zone of about 40,000 hectares in the basin, or more than one-third the overall surface area. ("Intertidal" means that sometimes an area is covered by seawater and sometimes it's exposed to the air.) Biologist Ed Bousfield comments: "No other coastal marine area in the world of comparable size has such a large proportion of bottom exposed to the air environment at low tide." This incredible natural phenomenon creates an environment in which life of many kinds can thrive.

comparative numbers reveal just how exceptional conditions are within the Minas Basin. At and near Grand Pré, tides typically rise and fall about 12 metres, twice each day, at twice the tidal range near the Annapolis Basin and seven times those between Halifax and Shelburne. It is predicted that the tidal ranges in the Minas Basin will continue to increase as global climate change accelerates the melting of the polar ice caps. In addition to a general rise in sea level, strong currents coming in and out of the Bay of Fundy are gradually deepening the Minas Basin, a development that will bring in steadily more water, intensifying the effect.

The waters of the Minas Basin, and those of the Bay of Fundy of which it is an offshoot, are incredibly muddy. The mud is the result of erosion, both of the Triassic-era sandstone cliffs that line the Basin's shores and that of the region's deep sea floor trenches. These chocolate-milk coloured waters are rich in nutrients, which are deposited in the silt of the wetlands of an intertidal zone and replenish what is required for abundant plant and marine life. If and when these wetlands are transformed into farmland—which

This photo of the northeast corner of Long Island shows the dramatic difference between the natural land–sea interface (lower half) and how it appears when an agriculturally minded people raise dykes and transform it (upper half) into highly productive arable land.

is what happened in the Acadian era and later during the Planter period—the nutrients developed in what was once a marine environment can be exploited for land-based farming. Such a transition was a remarkable accomplishment, rare in the history of seventeenth- and eighteenth-century North America. The land's resulting agricultural fertility, however, is only theoretical until the salt is removed from the top level at which crops are grown. This is what the Acadians would achieve and what the New England Planters would continue to exploit after the Acadians were forcibly expelled from the region in 1755.

Before we say any more about what the Acadians accomplished and how they did it, it is important to acknowledge that there were people living in the Grand Pré area long before the Acadians arrived. The original inhabitants were the Mi'kmaq. They too knew Grand Pré, though not by that name.

William H. Bartlett's mid-nineteenth-century engraving of the area near Annapolis reminds us that some Mi'kmaq were still living off the land in a seasonal round not so long ago. It was the government's twentieth-century centralization policies that would restrict Nova Scotia's Aboriginal people to a relatively small number of reserve areas.

CHAPTER 3

FIRST PEOPLES

*We believe that God gave us this land...we do not want the English living
in our land, the land we hold only from God. We will dispute that with all
men who want to live here without our consent.*

–LETTER ADDRESSED TO THE BRITISH ADMINISTRATION IN ANNAPOLIS
ROYAL, WRITTEN BY MI'KMAW CHIEFS AT OR NEAR
GRAND PRÉ, 1720

THE INDIGENOUS PEOPLE OF Nova Scotia were familiar with the
natural wetland at Grand Pré for thousands of years before any
Europeans arrived. We refer to the Mi'kmaq, though in the pre-
European era they called themselves *L'nuk* (meaning "the people").
Eventually, "Mi'kmaq" (also spelled "Micmac" and "Migmag")
came to be the name used to describe the people. As that happened, "Mi'kma'ki" became the term to describe the vast territory where the Mi'kmaq lived, in the Maritime provinces and
the Gaspé peninsula of Quebec.

   During that pre-European contact era, and for a long time
after, the Mi'kmaq followed what anthropologists call a "seasonal round." This essentially means that the Mi'kmaq—like

The Origin of "Mi'kmaq"

The term "Mi'kmaq" derives from a greeting early Europeans
heard the Mi'kmaq use: *nikmaq*. It meant "my family"; "my connections"; "my kin." Over time the "n" sound became an "m,"
and "Mi'kmaq" became the word used to identify the people, not
a relationship. In the orthography used by Mi'kmaq in today's
Nova Scotia, "Mi'kmaw" is the adjectival form and is used when
referring to a single person. The current orthography, known as
Smith-Francis after its developers, Douglas Smith and Bernie
Francis, dates from 1974.

23

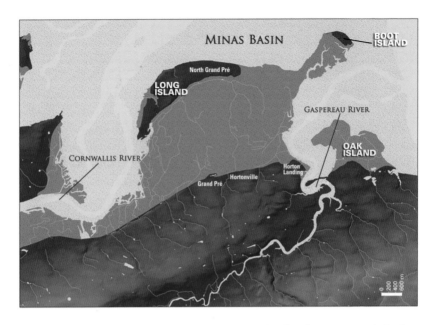

This illustration shows the full extent of what the Acadians accomplished at Grand Pré. Until they dyked the wetlands (shown in light green), those areas were twice each day fully or partly covered by seawater from some of the world's highest tides. This pre-dyking landscape was the one known to the Mi'kmaq before the Acadians arrived and began in stages to claim the wetlands from the sea.

the Wolastoqiyik (Maliseet) along the Saint John River and many other Aboriginal peoples in northeastern North America—travelled throughout the year to wherever food resources were available. Typically, the Mi'kmaq lived close to the coasts during the warm months and inland during the winter. Mi'kmaw place names often reflected a geographical characteristic of a location or the resources found there, for example, Musquodoboit, from the Mi'kmaw *Mooskudoboogwek*, meaning "suddenly widening out after a narrow entrance at the mouth" or "rolling out in foam," and Pugwash, derived from the Mi'kmaw *Pagweak*, meaning "deep water." Other examples of the precision and colour of Mi'kmaw, a member of the

H. N. Binney painted this scene about two centuries ago, presenting a way of life known to the Mi'kmaq for thousands of years.

Algonkian family of languages, are its names for the seasons. What English-speakers call May, the Mi'kmaq call *Tqoljewiku*, or "frog-croaking moon"; February is known as *Apiknajit*, "snow-blinder."

As for the Landscape of Grand Pré, Roger Lewis, Mi'kmaw archaeologist and curator of ethnology at the Nova Scotia Museum, confirms the existence of pre-Acadian place names. One was *Setnog* or *Chdnouk,* depending on the orthography, which translates as "extending out into the sea." This makes sense when we consider that before the Acadian transformation of the wetlands, the sea was present twice daily at Grand Pré between the mainland and Long Island. The second Mi'kmaw place name was *Galipotjegatiq*, meaning "little caribou place," for the area today known as Horton Landing. Presumably, this was a caribou crossing. Though caribou are now found only in more northern climes, Nova Scotia was home to an abundant population into the nineteenth century.

IN ANCIENT TIMES

Turning to the social and political organization of the Mi'kmaq many centuries ago, bands lived in separate districts, assembling occasionally in general councils to discuss matters that touched all. The usual interpretation is that by the time the Europeans first appeared off the coast of Atlantic Canada in the late 1400s and early 1500s—at first to fish, obtain furs, and explore—the Mi'kmaq saw their traditional territory in terms of seven distinct districts. These districts extended across much of what we think of as the Maritimes and into the Gaspé peninsula of Quebec. It is not known if they had firm geographical boundaries or varied according to the availability of resources in a given season. The shores of the Minas Basin were located in the *Sipekni'katik* district, or "wild potato area."

The ancient presence of the Mi'kmaq in what is known today as Kings County is best revealed through two sources: archaeological sites, and legends or oral traditions. There are at least sixty archaeological sites associated with the Mi'kmaq in the overall Grand Pré/Wolfville/Kingsport area, the largest concentration being along the Gaspereau River and at Gaspereau Lake. Melanson was one "traditional use" area, meaning a place where people camped and lived repeatedly over a long span of time. Some evidence found in this area dates back several thousand years. Other sites were "landing areas," meaning the places where Mi'kmaq regularly came ashore (or set off) when travelling over the waters of the Minas Basin to hunt, fish, or simply relocate for the season. One landing was on Long Island; another was beyond the western end of the Grand Pré Marsh, on the outskirts of Wolfville. During a 2009 survey of archaeology sites at Horton Landing, a team directed by Nova Scotia's provincial archaeologist Catherine Cottreau-Robins recovered near the water's edge a ground stone gouge that dates back nearly four thousand years; it's a powerful reminder that the area was known and used by Mi'kmaq long before any dyking began.

Archaeological excavations on the grounds of Fort Anne uncovered the prior Scottish fort of 1629–1632 known as Charlesfort. Among the artefacts uncovered were these ceramic pottery fragments (above) and projectile points (below) fabricated by the Aboriginal people with whom the Scots and French traded.

Leonard Paul's painting *Kluskap's Dancers* resonates with the rich traditions of storytelling and dancing in Mi'kmaw culture.

Mi'kmaw oral tradition is rich and complex. Perhaps the best-known figure of Mi'kmaw legends is Kluskap (Glooskap). A culture hero and key figure in Mi'kmaw creation myth, his adventures were recited and retold and contained valuable information for all who listened to them and passed them on. They subtly informed people about morality and of the respect that was needed for the environment and all creatures in it. The Minas Basin figures prominently in various Kluskap tales. It is important to realize that such legends were not just stories to while away an evening in front of a warming fire. According to Trudy Sable of the Office of Aboriginal and Northern Research at Saint Mary's University and Gerald Gloade of the Confederacy of Mainland Mi'kmaq, these legends also functioned as maps. These memorable tales contained vital geographical, geological, and environmental details, which taught listeners where to go to find different landmarks, food sources, or quarry sites. Because many Kluskap stories are situated in and around the Minas Basin, it is easy to imagine the Mi'kmaq

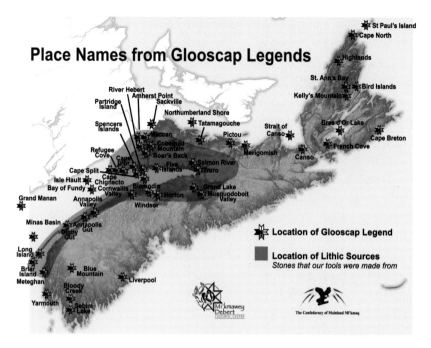

Place Names from Glooscap Legends

St Paul's Island
Cape North
Highlands
St. Ann's Bay
Bird Islands
River Hebert
Amherst Point
Sackville
Kelly's Mountain
Partridge Island
Northumberland Shore
Spencers Islands
Tatamagouche
Bras d'Or Lake
Pictou
Strait of Canso
Maccan
Merigomish
French Cove
Cape Breton
Refugee Cove
Cobequid Mountain
Boar's Back
Canso
Cape Split
Five Islands
Salmon River
Truro
Isle Hault
Cape Chignecto
Blomidon
Grand Lake
Bay of Fundy
Cornwallis Valley
Musquodoboit Valley
Grand Manan
Annapolis Valley
Horton
Windsor
Minas Basin
Annapolis Gut
Digby Gut
❋ Location of Glooscap Legend
Long Island
Briar Island
Blue Mountain
▊ Location of Lithic Sources
Stones that our tools were made from
Meteghan
Liverpool
Yarmouth
Bloody Creek
Sebim Lake

Mi'kmawey Debert CULTURAL CENTRE

The Confederacy of Mainland Mi'kmaq

This map of Nova Scotia produced by the Confederacy of Mainland Mi'kmaq shows how often place names along the Minas Basin cropped up in ancient Mi'kmaw Kluskap tales. It also reveals the areas from which rocks that could be used for tools (known as lithics) were mainly found.

travelling, camping, hunting, fishing, and quarrying stone in what we think of today as Kings, Colchester, and Cumberland Counties in Nova Scotia, and, of course, travelling over the saltwater basin that links them all. Beyond the Minas Basin lie other waterways and a broad land base that extends across the Maritimes and into Quebec, where the Mi'kmaq also lived (and still do).

In the previous chapter we mentioned Mi'kmaw legends that spoke of long-ago landscapes and geological or climate change. One researcher who has both listened closely to Mi'kmaw Elders and gone back to written accounts that date from centuries ago is Trudy Sable. She pioneered a close re-examination of the stories recorded by

Christian LeClercq, an early French missionary who lived among the Mi'kmaq in the Gaspé peninsula in the late 1600s. LeClerq heard tales about a great deluge that reminded him of the well-known Bible story of Noah's ark. The Mi'kmaw version similarly told of how there had once been a great inundation that flooded the world, accompanied by high winds. Many drowned as they tried to flee in their canoes. Only two people, a kind and virtuous man and a woman, survived. Thanks to them, the world was repopulated after the flood.

Later Europeans heard different Mi'kmaw accounts of the same cataclysmic event. In 1869 Baptist missionary Silas Rand recorded a story he heard from Mi'kmaw Elder Stephen Hood. "In former days, water covered the whole Annapolis Valley and Cornwallis Valley. Kluskap cut out a passage at Cape Split and at Annapolis Gut, and thus drained off the pond and left the bottom dry; long after this the valley became dry land." A generation or two later, the Capuchin missionary known as Father Pacifique (Henri Buisson de Valigny) summarized what he was hearing from other Mi'kmaq. In Father Pacifique's synopsis, Kluskap lived at Cape Blomidon in a very large wigwam and the Minas Basin was his beaver pond; that is, the basin was a lake separate from the Bay of Fundy. There was a dam running from Cape Split across to the Parrsboro shore. The Giant Beaver who created the dam and the lake behind it became overly proud, which prompted Kluskap to cut open the dam and flood the area.

These ancient Mi'kmaw stories, especially the last one, correspond to what oceanographers now confirm was the geological case before the barrier at the Minas passage gave way 3,000 to 4,000 years BP. This is a remarkable example of the scientific validation of an ancient oral tradition.

A HARMONIOUS RELATIONSHIP

In the long era before the 1680s, when Acadians arrived at Grand Pré, a vast intertidal zone lay between the upland and

Historical artist Francis Back depicts a small family group of Mi'kmaq returning to camp with food harvested. The style of clothing is that of the eighteenth century.

Long Island (then two kilometres offshore). To the Acadians, this zone was *la grand pré* ("the great marsh"). Seawater covered the lowest-lying portions twice a day and the higher areas less frequently, perhaps only during extreme high tides. It was a luxuriant salt marsh of over one thousand hectares with tidal drainage creeks, and home to a wide range of marine and estuarine life, including large numbers of birds and fish. The Mi'kmaq must have occasionally harvested a range of resources

Seasonal Visitors

The migratory birds that feast in the marsh creeks and on the mud flats near today's Grand Pré deserve a special mention. Recall that before the area was dyked and desalinated, these wetlands extended between the uplands and Long Island. The migratory birds that presently migrate to the area on a seasonal basis number in the millions. In late summer and early autumn, the air fills with the sights and sounds of huge flocks.

So important is the Minas Basin to many species of birds that, in 1988, the provincial and federal governments designated the area Canada's first Shorebird Reserve. The area is recognized internationally as a key migration stopover zone, especially for the semipalmated sandpiper (*Calidris pusilla*). The sandpipers fatten up in the Minas Basin before undertaking the seventy-two- to ninety-six-hour non-stop flight to South America. Before dyking began, Grand Pré had even more feeding areas for migrating birds than it does today.

A picture is worth a thousand words, or is that a thousand birds? Shown here are semipalmated sandpipers.

in that intertidal zone. Certainly, they did exactly that in other estuarine environments, making waterfowl, fish, shellfish, and sea mammals a part of their diet. At Grand Pré, before it was dyked, those species would have been abundantly available.

One naturally wonders what the Mi'kmaq thought when the Acadians began to transform intertidal zones into dykeland for agricultural purposes. It caused a dramatic change in the ecosystem. Yet there is no evidence that the Mi'kmaq objected to what the Acadians did—neither at Grand Pré nor anywhere else the Acadians carried out dyking projects. On the other hand, in 1720, Mi'kmaw chiefs assembled in the district of Les Mines (Minas), possibly at Grand Pré, and composed a strong letter, which they sent to British administration in Annapolis Royal, the gist being: "we do not want the English living in our land." This letter speaks volumes about the close and relatively friendly relationship between the Mi'kmaq and the Acadians.

What more commonly occurred upon the arrival of European peoples in the colonial era was conflict and confrontation between the Europeans and the original inhabitants of their prospective colonies. Countless lives were lost, and more often than not, Europeans displaced indigenous peoples in coastal areas. The Grand Pré Marsh, however, is a massive, one thousand-hectare artefact of evidence suggesting a relationship between European and Aboriginal peoples that was much more harmonious than the norm two and three hundred years ago. The great Acadian dyking project at Grand Pré, and the smaller ones elsewhere, could only have taken place with the consent and understanding of the Mi'kmaq, who greatly outnumbered the Acadians when these projects were first initiated. Moreover, the Mi'kmaq did not stop coming to Grand Pré (or to other Acadian settlements) after the Acadians settled there and the dyking began.

That the Mi'kmaq would accept the Acadian settlement and accompanying wetlands transformation is no small detail in our story. There are few examples in North American history of indigenous peoples and European (or European-descent) populations

Femme Acadienne.

Homme Acadien.

These late eighteenth-century images drawn by Grasset de Saint-Sauveur are identified as typical Acadians. This suggests there existed an uncertainty in the French as to where to draw the line between Acadians and Mi'kmaq.

accommodating each other as happened at Grand Pré and elsewhere in Acadie. A partial explanation for the harmony and understanding between the Mi'kmaq and Acadians was due to the two peoples sharing the same religion. Both groups were Roman Catholic. The Mi'kmaq had begun to adopt that faith at the Port-Royal habitation in 1610, where Chief Membertou and his family embraced Christianity. Most Mi'kmaq followed his example over the years, though many also retained their traditional spirituality, merging the two faiths. By the time the first Acadians settled at Grand Pré, the majority of Mi'kmaq were Catholic. In that era, a common religious faith provided an especially strong foundation for a close relationship between otherwise distinct peoples. (Differing religions, on the other hand, led to suspicion and sometimes hostility and warfare.)

C. 1900, Mi'kmaq still had at least a seasonal presence in the Grand Pré area.

Another important contributing factor to the amity between Acadians and Mi'kmaq was familial ties. Some intermarriage had occurred between French men and Amerindian women in the 1600s, and, though it occurred less often in the 1700s, the impact of these early mixed marriages was profound. Its effects are, indeed, still with us: today, many Acadian and Mi'kmaw family trees remain intertwined. An analysis of Acadian parish records between 1707 and 1748 reveals that about one-quarter of the population at Grand Pré were mixed-heritage individuals. Of all the many Acadian communities before 1755, Grand Pré was home to the highest percentage of mixed-heritage families.

The close relationship that emerged between the Mi'kmaq and the Acadians was certainly not unique to Grand Pré. It occurred at many other locations in Acadie and was undoubtedly a contributing factor in the Acadians' distinct identity. It is not possible to pinpoint exactly where or when it happened, but at some point during the latter half of the seventeenth century, the descendants of what had been mostly French colonists began to see themselves as a new people, *Acadiens* and *Acadiennes*.

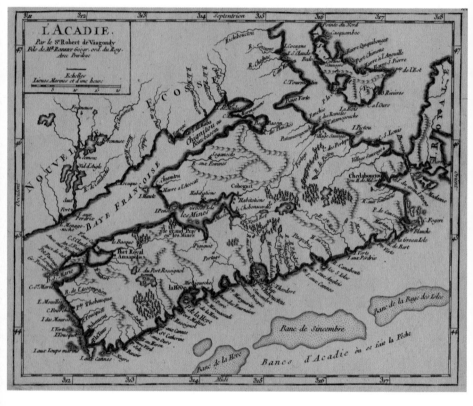

Mainland Nova Scotia (Acadie) as seen through the eyes of French map-maker Gilles Robert de Vaugondy in 1748. Grand Pré and other Acadian communities are named, but you'll have to look long and hard to find any English place names. Before the founding of Halifax in 1749, English colonists lived in only two small communities in Acadie/Nova Scotia: Annapolis Royal (formerly Port-Royal) and Canso (Canseau).

CHAPTER 4

THE ACADIAN ERA

*We cannot gaze upon the broad meadows before the door of Grand Pré
without remembering the hands that first held back the sea.*

–MARGARET W. MORLEY

THE LIFE OF GRAND PRÉ as an Acadian settlement began
in the early 1680s, a half-cen-
tury after the arrival of families from France gave Acadie
a solid foundation. The earlier phase—marked by the
early seventeenth-century adventures of Sieur de Monts,
Samuel de Champlain, Marc
Lescarbot, the Mi'kmaw chief
Membertou, and others—is
much better known. Yet that
phase ended definitively in 1613,
when Sir Samuel Argall's expedition from Virginia burned
the habitation at Port-Royal.

Though a few French
colonists remained in the region, Scots were the next to
settle at Port Royal, in 1629.
They dropped the hyphen and
established a small fortified
settlement at what are now the
grounds of Fort Anne National

This is artist Susan Tooke's rec-
reation of the earliest Acadian
settlers. The man and woman
depicted here represent the
Acadian generation prior to the
migration from the Port-Royal
area to Grand Pré.

Who Were the Acadians?

A variety of factors helped shape the original Acadian identity, producing a people who saw themselves as distinct from the French. Witnessing the independence of the Mi'kmaq must have been influential to the French, as was, undoubtedly, the degree of intermarriage between the two peoples, and the relative long-term isolation of the various Acadian communities from either French or British administrations. What administration existed was usually based at Port-Royal (later Annapolis Royal). By choosing to relocate away from the residences of government officials—to the Isthmus of Chignecto and along the Minas Basin—Acadians were able to greatly reduce any outside involvement in and control over their lives. Whether gaining control was a prime motivation for such relocations, or simply an effect caused by the desire to dyke and reclaim new fertile marshland areas is unknown.

Another influence was likely the natural setting in which the Acadians lived and worked. Just as they transformed the tidal marshes into farmland, so, too, their independent farming and fishing lives changed them. Thus, though French-speaking and Roman Catholic, over the course of the second half of the seventeenth century, the Acadians came to see themselves as belonging first and foremost not to France but to *l'Acadie* (which at the time coincided approximately to what we think of as mainland Nova Scotia).

Historic Site in Annapolis Royal. The Scottish venture, its headquarters within Charlesfort (also Charles Fort), was short lived. Yet it left behind the legacy of a Latin name for the colony (now province) of Nova Scotia ("New Scotland") as well as the inspiration for today's provincial flag and coat of arms.

When the Scots left Port Royal in 1632, the French returned to Acadie. This time, however, the initiative did not include adult males only: the French brought women and children, and put down roots. These roots would grow so deep, in fact, that a sizeable number of Acadians in the Maritimes today are the descendants of those French settler families. In 1632 the new French governor of Acadie, Isaac de Razilly, established a colony at La Have (La

Annapolis Royal has had a fortification of one sort or another since at least 1629, when the Scots erected Charlesfort. The French enlarged and improved the original fort, producing in 1701–02 the basic trace we see today. The British made only a few minor changes after they conquered Port Royal in 1710. It is from the British period that the name Fort Anne comes.

Hève), where he erected Fort Sainte Marie de Grâce. While Razilly was focused on developing La Have, he conceded Port-Royal to his brother, Claude de Launay-Razilly. The latter brother recruited new colonists to the area in 1636. A few were salt-workers (*sauniers*) from western France who were brought across the ocean "to make marshes" near Port-Royal. This transplanted *savoir faire* was going to make a huge difference throughout Acadie—particularly in the 1680s at Grand Pré, as we'll discuss later in this chapter.

The year the salt-workers arrived in the colony, Isaac de Razilly died. Charles de Menou d'Aulnay took over the control of the colony, and not long afterwards he relocated most of the Acadian population away from Nova Scotia's South Shore to Port-Royal,

In 1989 Parks Canada archaeologist Birgitta Wallace-Ferguson found this inscribed stone containing five lines of French, three of which are legible. It is the memorial stone for Joseph de Menou, eldest son of the seventeenth-century governor of Acadia, Sieur Charles de Menou d'Aulnay de Charnisay.

which he believed offered better prospects. When they arrived, the French colonists occupied the Scottish fort, built in 1629, and transformed it into one of their own. D'Aulnay would die from exhaustion and exposure after his canoe overturned in the cold water of the Annapolis Basin in May 1650. Yet he had left his mark as a major pioneer. He oversaw the construction of three forts, two mills, and two schools, and brought about twenty families to Acadie. Moreover, d'Aulnay continued the project, begun by Claude de Launay-Razilly, of erecting dykes and transforming intertidal zones into dry land for agriculture.

According to some sources, it is likely that the idea behind this transformation was, in the beginning, to create saltpans (shallow, artificial ponds of seawater which, through evaporation, produce

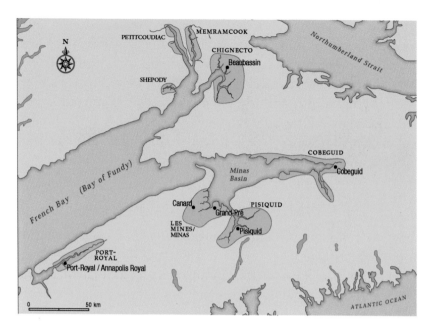

This map illustrates the major areas of Acadian settlement prior to the founding of Halifax in 1749. District names are in uppercase; individual villages are shown in a mix of upper- and lowercase.

salt) like those found on the west coast of France. Their creation would have given the settlers a reliable source of salt for the fishery and for other needs. That, however, is not how things played out. Instead, in the context of the wetland of Acadie, various intertidal zones were dyked and converted into land for agricultural purposes, rather than to obtain salt.

Between 1636 and 1670, the Acadian population and its dyking projects were based in the area of Port-Royal. Thereafter, there were several waves of Acadian out-migration from the area. Some Acadians were motivated by a desire for a fresh start in a new setting; others wanted to get away from the administration based at Port-Royal. Initial out-migration, between 1671 and 1672, was to the Isthmus of Chignecto region, with Acadians settling at what came to be known as Beaubassin. The next wave, a decade later, was to Grand Pré and other areas along the Minas Basin. There would be other waves later on, to Cobequid/Cobeguit (Truro) and Shepody/Chipoudie (Riverside-Albert, New Brunswick) in the early eighteenth century, and to Petcoudiac (Petitcodiac) and Memramcook a little later. Acadians also relocated to the French colonies of Île Royale (Cape Breton Island) and Île Saint-Jean (Prince Edward Island) between 1713 and 1757.

COMING TO GRAND PRÉ

Imagine coming to Grand Pré in the early 1680s, when what is now the reclaimed marsh was a vast wetland the Acadians called *la grand pré*, "the great marsh." (In today's international French, *pré* is masculine. In the 1600s, however—and for the many Acadians today who keep alive the seventeenth-century vocabulary and pronunciation—*pré* was feminine, hence *la*). The Acadians referred to the overall surrounding area of *la grand pré* as *Les Mines* (origin of the word "Minas"). This name dates back to the early 1600s and refers to the copper mines reputed to exist in the area, of which the Mi'kmaq had spoken to the first French explorers.

Though no mineral wealth was ever found at Les Mines, the name stuck, and the area found wealth of another sort. The Minas region, with Grand-Pré as its largest centre, became the principal agricultural centre and the granary of Acadie. This was to be achieved by altering, slowly but surely, what nature had provided. In a series of phases, the Acadians transformed the fertile intertidal zone, with its extremely high tides, into fertile agricultural land.

The Acadian settlement of Les Mines and area began when Pierre Melanson, *dit* "La Verdure," and his wife, Marie-Marguerite Mius d'Entremont, and their children relocated from Port-Royal to Grand-Pré. It is unknown where exactly they chose to live, but it may well have been in the vicinity of what we know today as Horton Landing. The Acadians called that particular area Vieux

Agriculture was a mainstay of Acadian communities. Sometimes they cleared the land of trees, but more commonly, and famously, they reclaimed marshland from the sea. The scene depicted here demonstrates how artist Azor Vienneau of the Nova Scotia Museum imagined the area at Belle Isle.

Logis, which literally translates as "Old Lodging." The name suggests that this area is, perhaps, where the Grand Pré community began, around 1682.

Around the same time that Pierre Melanson and Marie-Marguerite Mius d'Entremont were establishing themselves at Grand-Pré, Pierre Terriot and his wife, Cécile Landry, were founding a settlement of their own on the rivière aux Canards (Canard River). Meanwhile, Claude Landry and Catherine Thibodeau came to live along the rivière Saint-Antoine (Cornwallis River). All came from well-known Acadian families. Other Acadian settlers soon followed. Over the course of the next half century, many vibrant Acadian villages would grow up along the banks of the rivers and creeks that flowed into the Minas Basin: the rivière Sainte-Croix

The Melansons and the d'Entremonts

Wherever it was that Pierre and Marie-Marguerite came to live, both of their family names were already prominent in the history of Acadie. The Melanson family was one of the area's most well established and prosperous. Pierre's brother Charles remained, with his family, in the Port-Royal area, living only about 6.5 kilometres downriver, at Pointe-au-Chêne, also known as the village of Saint-Charles. Today it is a national historic site called the Melanson Settlement. Over time, Pierre Melanson emerged as the seigneurial agent, or *procureur fiscal*, for other families in the area of Les Mines. He also became a "captain of militia." In short, he was a leader of influence and authority.

The Mius d'Entremont family, too, had great prestige. The founder of the family line, Philippe Mius d'Entremont, was given the title "Baron de Pobomcoup" (Baron of Pubnico) in the 1650s by Governor Charles de Saint-Étienne de La Tour. The baron later became *procureur du roi*, lieutenant-major, and commander of the troops at Port-Royal. Marie-Marguerite, who came to Grand-Pré as the wife of Pierre Melanson, was one of the baron's children. In fact, the baron appears to have died at Grand-Pré in 1700, likely at his daughter's home. Marie-Marguerite was also related to the Saint-Étienne de La Tour family, which had claims over the seigneurie of Les Mines.

(St. Croix River), the rivière de l'Ascension or rivière Pigiguit (Avon River), the rivière Saint-Antoine, also called rivière des Habitants (Cornwallis River), the rivière "des Gasparots" (Gaspereau River), the rivière aux Canards (Canard River), and rivière des Vieux Habitants, or of the Vieille, or Old, Habitation (Habitant Creek). This last place name suggests the area was an early settlement of the Acadian period, beginning in the 1680s.

TRANSFORMING NATURE

Soon after their arrival, the Acadians began to transform *la grand pré* through a series of broad, community-based projects. How

A wood carving of Philippe Mius d'Entremont stands in front of the visitors' centre at the Village Historique Acadien de la Nouvelle-Écosse in West Pubnico.

the dyking of the intertidal zone was carried out is important. Their methods of wetland transformation distinguish the Acadian dykelands from the many others throughout world history, an aspect that contributed to the inscription of the Landscape of Grand Pré on the World Heritage list. We stated earlier that the great fertility of the dyked marsh at Grand Pré was a gift from nature. That it was, and the Acadians tapped into the natural fertility by enclosing and desalinating what nature provided. They did so by using techniques of wetland conversion, or land creation, they had perfected in the half century before there was any settlement at Grand Pré.

In the Port-Royal area, Acadian expertise with dyking intertidal zones dates back to the 1630s, when the Acadians who built them were given the nickname "*défricheurs d'eau*" ("land clearers of the sea"). Such an agricultural approach stood in sharp contrast to most other colonizing ventures in seventeenth- and eighteenth-century North America. European settlement patterns usually involved clearing away the forest then ploughing the land. And so it was back in Europe as well, where wetland tended to be transformed into agricultural land only as a last resort. That is, after all the best of the "dry" land was occupied or the fertility of those soils depleted. Exceptionally, the Acadians came to see that better productivity lay in the converted wetland of Acadie, rather than the uplands. They turned to the intertidal zones by choice, not out of necessity. In fact, the Acadians were the only pioneer settlers in colonial North America to farm extensively below the high-water mark.

The technology used to turn wetlands and marshes into farmland could not have been simpler: spades, pitchforks, axes, and a wooden sluice. But much more important than the tools was the ingenuity of the Acadian people. For starters, they had to read the natural drainage of the intertidal zones to first observe the direction and drainage of the creeks. The next challenge was to insert sluice boxes (hollowed-out logs or long plank boxes) near the bottom of the key creek beds—those that drained water. Supporting and keeping the sluice in place were poles, stakes, brush, and boughs. Recall that twice each day, the entire construction had to withstand incoming and outgoing tides, with seawater swirling around any

Aboiteau Origins

The origin of the term "aboiteau" lies in France. In the country's Atlantic coastal areas formerly known as Aunis and Saintonge, the word is spelled without the "i." And this was exactly how the French writer Dièreville spelled it in 1699 when describing dyking activities at or near Port-Royal during a visit to Acadie. The root of the word is *abot*, which signifies a dam or obstacle placed in water. In the Saintonge region, *abot* refers to a dam across a river, which reduces its flow, and/or a small earthen dyke dividing an oyster pond.

Obviously, this definition does not correspond to what we think of as an Acadian aboiteau, yet we can see how the older French term may have been transported and adapted in an Acadian context. The key element missing from *abot* is the valve or *clapet*, yet water-valves were used (and still are) in France for the control of the flowing water. They are known as water doors (*porte à flot* or *buses*). References to such techniques date back to well before the Acadians began their first dyking projects in the 1630s.

To transform the great marsh at Grand Pré the Acadians worked with the natural drainage system of numerous pre-existing creeks. With log piles, cribwork, dykes, and aboiteaux, the Acadians were able to reclaim the wetland by taking advantage of what nature provided.

incomplete work. It was an engineering accomplishment to outsmart the world's highest tides; yet it was vernacular engineering, because the Acadian farmers figured it out with little or no schooling. On their own, passing down techniques from generation to generation, the Acadians became masters of wetland transformation.

The first challenge faced by the Acadians was figuring out where to put the sluice. In the early years, hollowed-out tree trunks were used; later, handcrafted wooden boxes were specifically constructed. Either way, the sluice, or *dalle*, was placed at the bottom of a marsh's naturally flowing brook. The hinged clapper-end, essentially a check valve, faced the direction of the oncoming tidewater.

This painting by Lewis Parker shows how the Acadians went about placing their aboiteaux in the natural creek beds.

How the Acadian Aboiteau Worked

There are two essential parts to the Acadian aboiteau. One is the box or culvert (*la dalle*); the other is the dyke wall that surrounds and protects it. The key feature of the culvert is the hinged valve or *clapet* (clapper), which opens and closes automatically, depending on the direction of water flow. Water running off the enclosed dykeland can flow out through the *clapet*, but the seawater of a rising tide cannot come in. In the Acadian era, everything was built of wood. Today, every aboiteau is made of steel, but the principle behind it is the same.

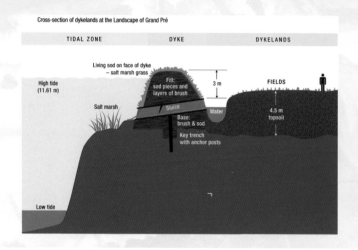

Cross-section of dykelands at the Landscape of Grand Pré

Next, an earthen levee or dyke was constructed over top. The entire assemblage or construction had to be anchored to withstand the rising and falling tides. Conifer boughs and clay from the marsh itself were added to the earthen embankment to strengthen it. While the sluice was placed in the brook, the earthen dyke lay across it at a right angle. If the work were done well, the complex would hold when the tidewater swirled around. The Acadians would return at the next low tide.

Gradually, they raised the earthen embankments to the left and right of the aboiteau in the natural brook. Once an entire area was completely closed off from the sea, no salt water could make

DRAINAGE SYSTEM USING AN ABOITEAU

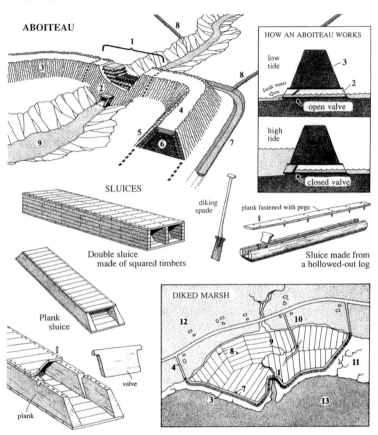

Legend: 1 – Aboiteau. This term designates not only the sluice but also the part of the dike which crosses the stream. Here, the dike is reinforced by fir trees laid transversally with alternate layers of clay soil. 2 – Sluice. 3 – Levee or dike. 4 – Road or path along the top of the dike. 5 – Dike facing made of sod. 6 – Earthen core (made of soil dug from the marshlands). 7 – *Contre-ceinture.* 8 – Drainage ditch. 9 – Stream. 10 – Road leading into the marshlands. 11 – Salt marsh. 12 – Dwellings on higher terrain. 13 – River or bay.

This illustration demonstrates how a generic aboiteau system works in relationship to the entire dyke.

Linguistic Details

Any linguists reading this book might be interested to know that in spoken Acadian, "aboiteau" is feminine while in written French it is masculine. It's yet another example of how languages change over time. Regardless of its gender, "aboiteau" has come to have two meanings. To some, it refers to the entire superstructure of sods, cribwork, and earth. Others use "aboiteau" to identify just a part of the whole, especially the box or culvert through which water passes.

it through the clapper valve. Only at low tide, when there was no pressure, would the clapper open, letting the rainwater or snow-melt from inside the dyked area run off.

One of the secrets to the Acadians' dyking success was in the material they used to construct earthen levees and aboiteaux: sods cut from the original wetlands. These were no ordinary grasses. They came from the natural wetland and could withstand being covered by salt water for many hours a day. They held fast because their deep and densely matted root systems kept them intact. Ordinary grasses, like those people use to grow their lawns, would have easily broken apart in the fast-flowing tidal waters of the Minas Basin. Sods that came from the marsh itself had very fine tidal silts deposited in the matrix of their roots. The two plants that consolidated the slopes of the dykes were *Spartina patens* and *Juncus gerardii*, especially on the outside slope, which felt the effects of the seawater.

Once an enclosed area was completed, the sea excluded, the next step was to drain and dry the former wetland to ready it for agriculture. Shallow ditches or drainage canals were dug, often in a rectilinear fashion in order to also mark off individual parcels of land. The various man-made canals interconnected and sloped gently, leading surface water to each aboiteau's closest naturally flowing brook. A deeper canal was dug just inside, running along the earthen embankment and facing the river or shoreline. It also led to the outlet where the sluice was located. With the drainage system in place, all Acadian farmers had to do was wait for

As this painting by Azor Vienneau depicts, in the era before modern earth-moving equipment the construction and maintenance of dykes required much ingenuity and many hands. It was a project to which the entire community contributed. All materials, such as sods, came from the immediate vicinity.

rainwater or snow to gradually wash the salt out of the top layers of soil in the enclosed area. Desalination generally took two to three years for each plot of dyked land, after which crops could be planted.

At Grand Pré, Acadians who wanted to reclaim the wetland first had to figure out three different drainage patterns. One flow pattern drained toward the Gaspereau River, another toward the Cornwallis River, and the third directly into the Minas Basin: easy enough to see in some areas, but tricky in others. It was essential to know the drainage direction of each portion of the vast marsh before building any aboiteaux, dykes, or surface canals. Ultimately, transforming the wetland was, for the Acadians, both an achievement of hydrological observation and one of arduous labour.

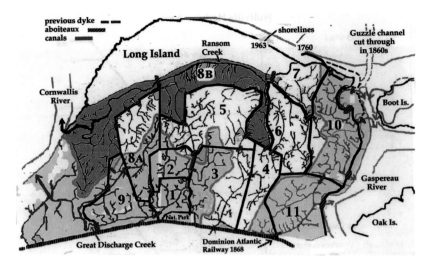

In this map, biologist and dykeland historian Sherman Bleakney shows the eleven-step sequence in which he suggests the intertidal zone was dyked. His hypothesis is based on the natural drainage of the creeks, physical evidence on the ground, and additional information provided by historical maps.

Because the Acadians did not have heavy, earth-moving equipment, they undertook wetland conversion in small, manageable phases. They appear to have begun with the "easiest" part of the marsh, parallel to the future site of the Memorial Church of Grand-Pré. Once that area was enclosed—and there arose a fresh need or desire for more highly fertile land—they moved on to enclose adjacent areas. It was an incremental approach that worked with nature, not against it.

Biologist and dykeland historian Sherman Bleakney has developed a plausible sequence of the dykeland enclosures. Whether or not dykeland transformation happened exactly as Dr. Bleakney suggests, is hard to say. Yet the authors of this book think he was close, if not precisely right. Gradually, over the span of seventy years, Acadian farm families turned nearly all of *la grand pré* into agricultural land. When they were forcibly removed in 1755, the

Every once in a while, farmers trenching with heavy equipment in the Grand Pré Marsh come across an old Acadian wooden sluice, part of a centuries-old aboiteau. The rescue archaeology operation depicted here took place in 2006.

Acadians left undyked only a portion at the western limit of the wetland. The descendants of the New England Planters would successfully undertake that project at a later period.

The transformation of wetland into dykeland at Grand Pré eventually added up to about one thousand hectares. It can be thought of as a massive artefact: a living testament to the original Acadian accomplishment and to the subsequent stewardship of the New England Planters as well as those who came later. What was achieved at Grand Pré was the largest dyking project completed anywhere in Atlantic Canada before 1755. Not only that, but it was completed in the context of some of the highest recorded tides in the world and was accomplished in a community-based manner. The latter is an important distinction, as similar projects in Europe were generally organized and implemented from the top down.

As discussed earlier, the Acadian villages did not feel the impact of much governance. They largely administered themselves. For a

The Criterion (v) Argument

UNESCO found that the Landscape of Grand Pré met the requirements of Criterion (v) of the World Heritage Convention in the following manner:

Criterion (v): The cultural landscape of Grand Pré bears exceptional testimony to a traditional farming settlement created in the 17th century by the Acadians in a coastal zone with tides that are among the highest in the world. The polderisation used traditional techniques of dykes, aboiteaux and a drainage network, as well as a community-based management system still in use today. The resultant rich alluvial soil enabled continuous and sustainable agricultural development.

dyking project to be undertaken, many people had to be involved. The decision to take part and support the work came from those living in the area. The community-based approach to the ownership of the Grand Pré Marsh continued after the Acadians were exiled, and still exists. Today it is the farmers who own the individual lots on the marsh, known collectively as the Grand Pré Marsh Body, who make the decisions. This quality contributed to UNESCO's finding the Landscape of Grand Pré a place of "outstanding universal value" under Criterion (v) of the World Heritage Convention.

A GROWTH CENTRE

The fertility of the Grand Pré Marsh, once dyked and desalinated, was remarkable. (The cleared uplands alongside the dykeland were also fertile, but in comparison were much less productive than the converted intertidal zone.) Once word of the marshland's fertility spread, more Acadians were attracted to the area. In-migration, along with high birth and survival rates, caused the population to expand. As a result, the settlement at Grand Pré expanded along the uplands adjacent to the great marsh. It had no grid, but extended as people settled from (today's) Hortonville all the way to Wolfville. The community included houses, farm buildings,

Claude Picard's painting of a harvest scene at Grand Pré. Note the windmill in the background.

orchards, gardens, storehouses, windmills, and the parish church of Saint-Charles-des-Mines. French commandant Joseph Robinau de Villebon noted, during a 1699 visit to the area, that he had seen one windmill and seven or eight water mills.

Within a few decades, Grand Pré became the most populous Acadian settlement. Both the growth and relative prosperity of the area were linked to the exceptional fertility of the intertidal zone-turned-agricultural land. It was not long before the Acadians of Grand Pré were producing more than they could consume. They began to sell their surplus, especially grain, to buyers in both French and British settlements, such as Louisbourg and New England, in the 1730s and 1740s. Historians who refer to the "Golden Age" of the Acadians (1713–44) reference the growth of Grand Pré as evidence of that bountiful, peacetime era. After the founding of

Past where the Deportation Cross now stands at Horton Landing, out on the Gaspereau River, vessels came and went according to the tides. They often brought manufactured items and sailed away with Acadian foodstuffs.

Halifax in 1749, Grand Pré's surplus was sold to help feed that growing town as well.

The exports from Les Mines were shipped away in vessels that anchored in the Minas Basin. Barrels and bales were loaded along the Gaspereau River at what was then referred to as Vieux Logis and is now known as Horton Landing. This was the "port" for Grand Pré, where exports left and imports—ceramics, tools, fabric, and so on—arrived. That same landing area would later become the last firm ground upon which most of the area's Acadians would walk before being sent into exile in 1755. And it would be there, in 1760, that hundreds of New England Planters would make landfall before taking over the region. But we are getting ahead of our story. It is time now to turn to the troubled history of the same area, the tragic, second rationale behind the World Heritage designation of the Landscape of Grand Pré.

Susan Tooke's artwork produced for the visitors' centre at Grand Pré National Historic Site sums up the dilemma facing the Acadians in the years leading up to mass deportations that began in 1755. The Acadians were caught in an impossible situation between two rival empires, symbolized by the soldiers of Great Britain (left) and France (right).

CHAPTER 5

TIMES OF TROUBLE

About three in the morning the Enemy Attackt us. It Stormed with Snow at that time....They knew all our Quarters & the numbers Station'd in every House.

–CHARLES MORRIS, ENGLISH OFFICER, 1747

THE FRENCH COLONIZATION OF Acadie did not take place in a vacuum. There were political and military contexts surrounding events and developments throughout the Americas. Beginning in the late fifteenth century, first hundreds and then thousands of European mariners and colonists—Spanish, Portuguese, French, English, Dutch, Scottish, Swedish, and others—crossed the North and South Atlantic. The three most common reasons for those ventures and voyages were to expand commerce, to establish new settlements, and to disseminate a particular religious faith. The colonization of the Maritimes, first by the French and later by the Scottish and English, was part of a vast international phenomenon.

From the early seventeenth to the mid-eighteenth century, this region, known alternatively as Mi'kma'ki, Acadie, and Nova Scotia, witnessed conflicts among various groups and interests. It was during this same era that Acadians were establishing their communities and building dykes to reclaim marshes, including the one at Grand Pré. The villages along the Minas Basin felt the impacts of several conflicts.

In 1696 and 1704, wartime expeditions from New England led by Benjamin Church arrived in different parts of Acadie. The first attack came during the nine-year European conflict known as the War of the League of Augsburg (or King William's War in the Anglo-American colonies). Church's focus then was on the Acadian settlement at Beaubassin, which

This medal commemorates the 1713 Treaty of Utrecht, which shifted the European allocation of sovereignty in the Maritimes. The treaty gave mainland Nova Scotia to Great Britain and Cape Breton Island (Île Royale) and Prince Edward Island (Île Saint-Jean) to France. The Mi'kmaq, the original inhabitants of the region, were neither signatories, nor even at the table.

he largely destroyed. In the second episode, which took place during the War of the Spanish Succession (or Queen Anne's War), the attackers came to Grand Pré. There, in 1704, they burned houses, carried off prisoners, and broke the dykes to let in seawater. According to a contemporary account, the soldiers dug "down the dams [dykes], and let the tide in, to destroy all their corn, and everything that was good." Once the expedition left, the Acadians returned to the area and set out once again to re-establish themselves. That would mean rebuilding their houses and repairing their dykes. Recall that it would take another two to three years for the salt from the seawater to leach out of the marshland soil.

The war ended with the Treaty of Utrecht (1713), whose terms of the peace included the transfer of sovereignty over Acadie to Great Britain. Truth be told, however, though it wasn't recognized right away, what the French meant by Acadie was not what the

British understood to be Nova Scotia. Practical limits or boundaries were not specified. And nowhere was the misunderstanding more important than in the Isthmus of Chignecto. Both France and Britain thought the area was "theirs," and neither imperial power considered the millennia-long occupation of the entire region by the Mi'kmaq meant that the area's indigenous people had a stake in the discussion. The confusion over where sovereignty and jurisdiction began and ended in the Chignecto area ultimately led to the total upheaval of the Acadian world, to which we'll return later on.

When the Treaty of Utrecht was signed, the British presence in Nova Scotia was small. There were few British settlers and only two tiny garrisons, at Annapolis Royal and Canso. The rest of the territory was either known only to the Mi'kmaq or home to Acadian villages. The Acadian population at this time numbered about 2,400 souls. Historian William Wicken estimates that the Mi'kmaw population was a similar figure as well. By the eve of the Deportation, four decades later, that Acadian population had grown nearly sevenfold. Genealogist Stephen White calculates that in 1755 there were slightly more than 14,000 Acadians living in the Maritimes.

THE LOYALTY QUESTION

In 1713, with the Acadian population relatively small, British officials wondered what to do with the former French colonists. (Rarely did the British call them Acadians; more common were "Inhabitants," "French Inhabitants," or "French Neutrals.") British officials worried that these subjects might not give their full allegiance to the British monarch. Instead, might they assist and fight for the French if there was another war? And, as the history of the past century had shown, there was always another war. The concern magnified as years went by, and played the determining role in the events that led to the forcible removal of Acadians throughout the region beginning in 1755.

A Misunderstanding Over Oaths

In 1729–30, Acadians on mainland Nova Scotia thought they had reached a solution to the British demand for an oath of loyalty. They agreed to a modified oath proposed by Governor Richard Philipps, based at Annapolis Royal, who gave a verbal assurance that the Acadians would not be required to take up arms against the French or the Mi'kmaq. They could remain neutral.

Unfortunately for the Acadians and the British governor, a modified oath was not something the authorities in Great Britain would accept. Events in the 1740s and 1750s led subsequent British administrations—especially after Halifax was founded and became the capital of Nova Scotia in 1749—to revisit the question of Acadian allegiance. From 1749 on, the British insisted ever more strongly that the Acadians swear the customary oath of loyalty expected of conquered or colonized peoples without exception, with no possibility of neutrality. Painting below is by Nelson Surette.

At Grand Pré and elsewhere, Acadians mostly tried to remain outside the loyalty debate and aloof from the imperial rivalry between France and Great Britain. Tragically for the Acadians, such a "neutral" stance was unacceptable to officials on both sides. The French believed that a common religion, language, and descent should make Acadians loyal to their king. The British, however, like other Europeans of the era, saw the Acadians as subjects of the monarch who, on paper at least, ruled over them. The reality on the ground, in most historians' eyes, is that while there were some pro-French Acadians as well as others who worked with the British, the vast majority was caught in the middle, wishing for the imperial rivalry to fade away.

IMPERIAL WARS

After nearly three decades of peace, Great Britain and France found themselves again at war. This time it was the War of the Austrian Succession (1740–48). Europe was the main theatre, but Atlantic Canada also saw hostilities. Several incidents occurred at or near Grand Pré.

In the summer of 1744, a military expedition from the French stronghold at Louisbourg advanced through the main Acadian communities. The officer in command, François Du Pont Duvivier, had been born at Port-Royal prior to its capture by the British in 1710. At Beaubassin, Grand Pré, and other Acadian villages, Duvivier appealed to men to join his campaign. Few answered the call, preferring to stay out of the conflict. Also, there was a harvest to bring in. The overall Acadian response disappointed Duvivier and the French leadership at Louisbourg. They had expected and wanted active participation. The British, however, saw it as a major disappointment that the Acadians had allowed the French force to advance through their communities without rising up against them or warning the British. The Acadians were caught in the middle of an impossible dilemma: trying to stay neutral when armed conflict is underway.

The following year, 1745, the French attacked Annapolis Royal. Around the same time, supported by British warships, an army of provincial New England soldiers captured Louisbourg. In 1746 France outfitted a massive expedition commanded by the naval officer the Duc d'Anville to sail across the Atlantic on a mission to regain Louisbourg, capture Annapolis Royal, and compel the Acadians to commit themselves to the French cause. The expedition ended in disaster due to delays, storms, and illnesses, but what *might* have happened underlined to the British the vulnerability of their hold on Nova Scotia.

Though the 1746 expedition from France was a failure, a ground force from Canada (today's Quebec)—about 250 French soldiers and 50 Amerindian allies—came into the Acadian communities to give support. That force withdrew to Beaubassin in the Chignecto region after the naval flotilla dispersed to France. Soon after, in the fall of 1746, about 500 New England soldiers under the command of Col. Arthur Noble arrived in Grand Pré to establish a military presence. These Anglo-American troops took over numerous Acadian houses at Grand Pré and planned to launch an attack the following spring against the enemy overwintering at Beaubassin. When the French and Amerindian force heard that the New Englanders were at Grand Pré, they decided, despite being outnumbered in mid-winter, to attack.

With Nicolas-Antoine Coulon de Villiers in charge, the French and Amerindian force set out for Grand Pré in January 1747. They were joined or assisted by a small number of Acadians. At the same time, pro-British Acadians warned the New England soldiers an attack could be imminent. The New England troop ignored the warnings, thinking the severe winter conditions would protect them. The result is known to history as the Battle of Grand Pré.

In the early morning hours of February 11, 1747, in the middle of a blinding snowstorm, an outnumbered French and Amerindian force completely surprised the approximately five hundred New England soldiers installed in twenty-four houses at Grand Pré. Most were in bed. The encounter left between seventy and one hundred New Englanders dead, including the commander, Col. Arthur Noble. Another fifty soldiers were taken prisoner. On the other side, only seven French and Amerindians were killed. Eight

Renowned historical artist C. W. Jefferys (1869–1951) captures the drama of the 1747 nighttime battle at Grand Pré, carried out in a snowstorm between a French and Amerindian force and a contingent of soldiers from New England.

years later, in 1755, the incident loomed large in the thinking of British leaders who insisted on a mass removal of all Acadians.

The War of the Austrian Succession ended in late 1748, and the Treaty of Aix-la-Chapelle returned Atlantic Canada to its previous status quo: Louisbourg and the colonies of Île Royale (Cape Breton Island) and Île Saint-Jean (Prince Edward Island) were again French. Not long after, both France and Britain took unprecedented military action in Atlantic Canada. France sent an expedition of several thousand colonists to reoccupy Louisbourg and soon established a post at the mouth of the Saint John River and Forts Beauséjour and Gaspareaux (Gaspereau) in the Chignecto region.

Commemorating the Battle of Grand Pré

In 1924 the Historic Sites and Monuments Board of Canada (HSMBC) found the 1747 Battle of Grand Pré to be an event of national significance. It was the first "national" commemoration erected at Grand Pré. Though the graves of Col. Noble and others are no longer clearly marked, there still remains a monument to the battle. It consists of twin HSMBC plaques and can be found where the Old Post Road intersects the Grand Pré Road.

The British were even more ambitious: First, they sent a massive expedition to found Halifax as a counterbalance to Louisbourg. Then, over the next few years, they erected posts, forts, and settlements to expand their power beyond Halifax. These included Fort Edward in the Acadian community of Pisiquid (Windsor), a small fort at Vieux Logis (Horton Landing) near Grand Pré, Fort Lawrence (prior to and opposite Fort Beauséjour), and a brand new town of "foreign Protestants" at Lunenburg. With a much stronger presence on the ground, the British administration in Halifax revisited the old question of Acadian neutrality. But this time they did so with a determination to settle the matter once and for all. Gone was the relatively weak position of their predecessors at Annapolis Royal.

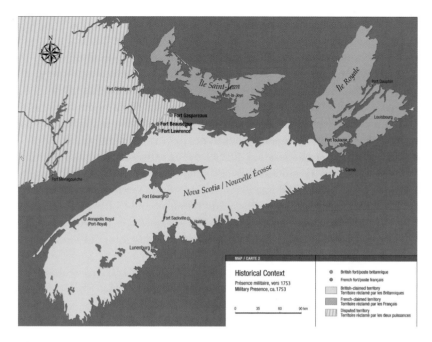

This map sums up the situation in the Maritimes as it stood in the mid-eighteenth century, from a European perspective. Missing from the depiction is the important presence of the Mi'kmaq. Because they moved seasonally and did not erect towns or forts, their presence is not easy to reflect on such a map.

What came next is known to history as the Acadian Deportation. We do not have the space in this book to explore all nuances of the subject, but we do want to make a few points. First, the singular term "Acadian Deportation" encompasses the many separate forcible removals of Acadians from what are now the Maritime provinces over a period of seven years, beginning in 1755. In the end, about three-quarters of the slightly more than fourteen thousand Acadian men, women, and children then living in the Maritime region were deported to destinations in North America or Europe. The others went into hiding or fled to locations they hoped would be safe.

Le Grand Dérangement

By this term, used increasingly in English, we refer to the sweeping series of events that occurred in Nova Scotia/Acadie in the mid-eighteenth century. It's not a term invented by historians, but one Acadians themselves used at the time. The authors of this book apply the term more broadly than many other historians. We suggest that the Grand Dérangement began not in 1755 but at the founding of Halifax in the summer of 1749—soon after which, a portion of the Acadian population in Mirligouèche (later Lunenburg) and Chezzetcook felt it had to relocate to French territory on Cape Breton Island. Acadians in Pisiquid (Windsor) and Cobeguit (near Truro) did the same in the spring of 1750. Meanwhile, nearly a thousand Acadians at Beaubassin found themselves forcibly relocated by French orders in 1750.

As you can see, several years before 1755, nearly a quarter of the Acadian population was already "*dérangé*" or "upset." And the "great upheaval" did not end when the Deportation officially stopped in 1762. Many Acadians would remain unsettled and on the move until the early nineteenth century.

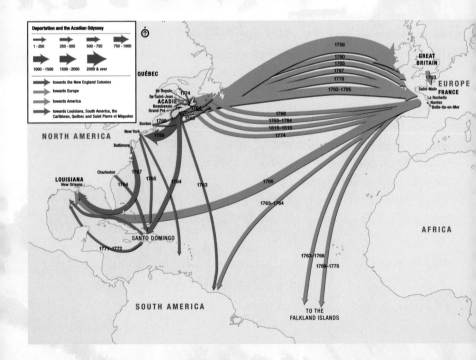

WARFARE AND FATEFUL DECISIONS

What unfolded at Grand Pré in 1755 began a few hundred kilometres away, with a British military expedition to the Chignecto Isthmus. In late 1754 and early 1755, the acting governor of Nova Scotia, Charles Lawrence, collaborated with Massachusetts Governor William Shirley. Together, they organized a large military expedition, which brought about two thousand Anglo-American provincial soldiers and three hundred British regulars to Nova Scotia. Overall command was given to British officer Lt.-Col. Robert Monckton. The expedition's goal was to capture Forts Beauséjour and Gaspareaux, eliminating the French military from the region. War was not declared between Great Britain and France until the spring of 1756—but warfare already existed between the two sides, in the Ohio Country and on the high seas.

Using Fort Lawrence as its base, the Monckton-led expedition accomplished its goal quickly in June 1755: the attackers outnumbered defenders about ten to one. The captured French fort became Fort Cumberland, while the surrendered Fort Gaspareaux became Fort Monckton. When word reached the administration in Halifax that two to three hundred Acadians had participated in the defence of Fort Beauséjour, acting governor Charles Lawrence and the Nova Scotia Council were not pleased. They discounted completely the French commander's affirmation that he had compelled the Acadians to participate on pain of death. In the eyes of the British officials, the mere presence of Acadian defenders within the French fort was a sign of complicity.

In short order, Lawrence and the Council resolved that all Acadians in the Chignecto region be rounded up and deported. It was a sweeping decision that ignored any requirement to prove the involvement of particular individuals. It was kept completely secret, known to no one outside the council room. Surveyor general Charles Morris had already prepared a report the year before, describing in great detail each Acadian community in the region

The French fort atop Beauséjour ridge was only a few hundred metres away from British Fort Lawrence on Beaubassin ridge. In between the two lay a great marsh and the Missaguash River.

and a suggested stratagem for its removal from the colony. Morris's report essentially offered a blueprint for the Acadian Deportation.

On July 28, 1755, after meeting twice with the deputies of the Acadian communities in mainland Nova Scotia, the Nova Scotia

Council took its as yet unannounced policy one major step further: it resolved to remove *every* Acadian—men, women, and children—from *all* of Nova Scotia, not just Acadians in the Chignecto region. The new policy was first implemented in August 1755, when all Acadian males were summoned to Fort Cumberland for what was said to be an important announcement. No hint was offered as to what it would mean to the Acadians. Once inside the gates, the summoned males were imprisoned. It would be months later, once the necessary ships had arrived, before they would be transported, with or without their families, to the Anglo-American colonies. A wider implementation of the deportation policy would begin at Grand Pré and nearby Pisiquid in early September 1755.

GRAND PRÉ, 1755

Though the Acadian Deportation was a political and military event, it also had an economic dimension. British officials in Halifax were fully aware of the fertility and agricultural value of the Acadians' land, at Grand Pré and elsewhere. On October 18, 1755, Charles Lawrence wrote to the Lords of Trade in London, England, reinforcing the importance of continuing to cultivate the Acadian dykelands. He stated: "As soon as the French are gone, I shall use my best endeavours to encourage People from the Continent to settle their lands…and the additional circumstances of the Inhabitants evacuating the Country will, I flatter myself, greatly hasten this event, as it furnishes us with a large Quantity of good Land ready for immediate Cultivation."

Of all the forcible removals of the Acadians, the one at Grand Pré is by far the best known. This is largely due to the detailed accounts left behind by a few of the New England officers involved. One of these stands above the rest, the journal written by John Winslow. Lt.-Col. John Winslow of Massachusetts was the officer in charge of rounding up and deporting the Acadians from Grand Pré. He arrived in the village on August 19, 1755, with about three hundred New England provincial soldiers. All had taken part in the capture of Fort Beauséjour. This was their next assignment. As the British officers had done in the Chignecto region, Winslow gave no indication to the Acadians in the Minas area what was going to happen. On the contrary, he gave the impression he was there on routine business. First, he established a secure base of operations by erecting a palisade enclosing the church of Saint-Charles-des-Mines, the priest's house, and the cemetery— a precaution undertaken because his 300-man force was greatly outnumbered by the 2,200 Acadian men, women, and children in the Minas Basin area. Winslow's troops pitched their tents within the enclosed area. So as not to provoke the Acadians unnecessarily, Winslow asked community leaders to remove any sacred objects from the church before it became a military base.

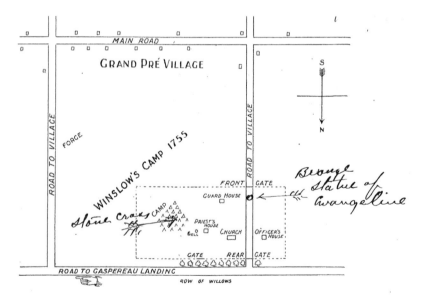

In 1900 John Frederic Herbin came up with this plan to show how he thought Lt.-Col. John Winslow's camp was laid out at Grand Pré. For orientation, a later hand (probably Herbin himself) identified where the Evangeline Statue and Herbin Cross were erected.

As August came to a close, the Acadians of Grand Pré and nearby villages were busy harvesting crops from the marshland and cultivated upland areas. Unbeknownst to them, this would be their last harvest in these surroundings. On September 4, 1755, Lt.-Col. Winslow issued a call for all males in the Grand Pré area aged ten and older to come to the parish church at three o'clock in the afternoon on the following day to hear an announcement. It was the same approach used at Fort Cumberland a month earlier. Winslow had been there and seen how well the stratagem had worked—and no one had escaped to warn other Acadians. At Fort Edward in Pisiquid, Capt. Alexander Murray issued the same order on the same day as Winslow.

On September 5, as requested, 418 Acadian men and boys of Grand Pré proceeded to their parish church, now surrounded by a palisade and controlled by armed soldiers, for the announcement. Once inside, Winslow's French-speaking interpreters informed the males, "that your Lands and Tenements, Cattle of all Kinds and Live Stock of all Sorts are Forfeited to the Crown with all of your Effects Saving your money and Household Goods and you your Selves to be removed from this…Province." One eyewitness, another New Englander, recorded that the look on the Acadian faces as they heard the announcement was a mixture of "shame and confusion…together with anger"; their "countenances" so altered they could not be described.

The removal of the more than two thousand Acadians living at Grand Pré and in the neighbouring Minas Basin villages did not proceed quickly or smoothly: there was a shortage of transport ships and a lack of provisions. The imprisoned men and boys would end up spending more than a month either inside the church or on transports anchored in the Minas Basin. Eventually, the entire population would be forced on board the ships.

On October 8, 1755, the embarkation of the men, women, and children to the waiting ships began, with the small vessels setting off from Horton Landing. Those living at Grand Pré and

A number of artists have depicted the devastating impact the reading of the Deportation announcement had on those inside the church at Grand Pré on September 5, 1755. This is the interpretation of Acadian artist Claude Picard.

Gaspereau went first. Winslow wrote that the inhabitants left "unwillingly, the women in Great Distress Carrying off Their Children in their Arms, Others Carrying their Decrepit Parents in their Carts and all their Goods moving in Great Confusion

In Winslow's Own Words

Winslow described the first contingent of young men marching along the road beside the dyked marshland, heading for Horton Landing, in these words: they "went off Praying, Singing, & Crying, being Met by the women & Children all the way…with Great Lamentations upon their knees praying."

George Craig's 1893 painting *Expulsion of the Acadians* is a sweeping, highly detailed work. The background shows the **community's** vast reclaimed marshland, with smoke from the buildings set ablaze. The foreground **depicts** the church and palisade within which the men and boys were detained, and the rest of the community in upheaval. That the artist dresses the soldiers in blue is not a mistake: in 1755 **New England** soldiers, not British redcoats, were most responsible for carrying out the Deportation.

and appeared a scene of Woe and Distress." Winslow ordered that families be kept together, yet in the confusion that was not always possible. Moreover, Acadian families included more than a mother, father, and children; there were grandparents, in-laws, aunts, uncles, cousins, nephews, and nieces. Friends, relatives, and neighbours were sometimes separated, never to see each other again.

On October 19–21, the New England soldiers forced families from the outlying communities to assemble at Grand Pré in preparation for boarding the transport ships. This time the departure point was not Horton Landing but Budrot Point (Starrs Point),

This piece by Susan Tooke features the poignant moment when those Acadians aboard the departing ships were sailing out of the Minas Basin for destinations, to them, unknown.

located between the Canard River (to the north) and the Habitants or Cornwallis River (to the south). While awaiting the arrival of the transports, the group of about 600, from 98 families, lodged in the recently vacated homes of the people of Grand Pré. Three hundred fifty of this group were sent away on December 13; the remainder a week later. They had been preceded by more than 1,500 inhabitants of Grand Pré and the Gaspereau River area and more than 1,000 inhabitants from Pisiquid who'd been sent away in mid-October. Everywhere, children made up the largest category.

Once the Acadians were on board, the transport ships set sail for Connecticut, Maryland, Massachusetts, Pennsylvania, and

The First Cajuns

No Acadians were deported directly to Louisiana during the period between 1755 and 1762. That's because Louisiana was then a colony of France. However, beginning in 1765, at which time Louisiana had become a Spanish colony, Acadians who had been deported to the British colonies further north began to migrate to French-speaking, Roman Catholic Louisiana. Many more would relocate there later on, becoming "Acadians of the South" or Cadjens (Cajuns). The first Acadian arrival is depicted in this painting by Louisiana artist George Rodrigue.

Virginia. In total, approximately 2,100 Acadians were deported from the Minas area in 1755, accounting for roughly one-third of the 5,800 Acadians deported from Nova Scotia during the first year of forcible removals.

THE VILLAGE LEFT BEHIND

The soldiers who carried out the various roundups and removals in 1755 had orders to burn the houses, barns, churches, and all other structures the Acadians had built. The idea was that there would be no shelter for anyone who might have escaped. According to Winslow's journal, soldiers set fire to 698 buildings in the Grand Pré region: 276 houses, 255 barns, 155 outhouses, 11 mills, and 1 church. The village of Grand Pré itself, however, was spared—at least initially: it was where Winslow had his headquarters. These buildings later housed the approximately six hundred Acadians from Budrot (Starrs) Point until they, too, were shipped off.

With a simple yet powerful composition, Nelson Surette's *Burn* effectively communicates how soldiers set about to systematically eliminate every building the Acadians had erected in their many communities.

Some of the structures at Grand Pré may have been burned after December 1755. Certainly, at least some survived. Surveyor General Charles Morris wrote that roughly one hundred buildings still stood at Grand Pré when the Planters arrived in the spring of 1760. One such building was likely the parish church of Saint-Charles-des-Mines; a description of the Acadian church exists in the oral tradition of some Planter family descendants.

The Acadian Deportation is one of the best-known tragedies in Canadian, even North American history. Countless artistic, historical, literary, and musical works convey what happened, what

Acadian Odyssey memorials found in Canada, the United States, and France mark the many forced migrations of Acadians over the second half of the eighteenth century. The Deportation Cross of Grand Pré is the evocative symbol used on each one. Depicted here is the memorial on the Halifax waterfront, in view of Georges Island, where many Acadians were held prisoner during the Deportation.

it meant, and how it must have felt. Without question, the location most closely associated with the Deportation is Grand Pré, thanks initially to the detailed account left behind by John Winslow. But there are other reasons why Grand Pré emerged as the pre-eminent site, which we discuss in chapter 7. Before that, we turn our attention to the group who took over the stewardship of the entire Grand Pré area after the tragedy of 1755.

C. W. Jefferys depicts the 1760 arrival of the New England Planters in Nova Scotia in an idealized manner. It seems unlikely they streamed off the ships quite like this, neither quite so nattily dressed nor with such broad smiles. They had an enormous workload ahead before successfully settling in their new land.

CHAPTER 6

THE COMING OF THE NEW ENGLAND PLANTERS

The coast of the Bay of Fundy is unquestionably the garden of Acadia.
–JOHN YOUNG ("AGRICOLA"), 1822

BY THE END OF 1755, Grand Pré was an abandoned landscape. The highly fertile dykeland and its adjacent upland, where Acadians had lived for over seventy years, lay dormant and silent: no new crops planted, no animals raised, no one looking after the dykes to protect the valuable marshland. It was only a matter of time before nature began to reclaim what the Acadians had created and cultivated.

THE STORM OF 1759

In November 1759 an event known to scientists as a Seros-cycle maximum high tide struck. It is an event that occurs every 18.03 years in the Bay of Fundy and Minas Basin, generating much higher than normal tidal amplitudes. In 1759 it arrived at the same time as a great storm. The twin effects caused a massive sea surge that breached the dyke walls at Grand Pré in several places alongside the Gaspereau River. The high water flooded a large portion of the dykeland. Seawater would have covered its entirety, formerly a flat intertidal zone, had the Acadian dykes on the interior sections—those claimed from the sea before the Acadians tackled and enclosed the outlying portions—not held firm. The storm event also meant that submerged portions of the dykeland would return to something resembling their original tidal marsh condition. And so it would have been, had not a new group arrived in the area soon after. Those settlers, Planters from New England, made it a priority to repair or rebuild the old Acadian dykes. As a result, it was not long before the agricultural use of Grand Pré began anew, this time with people of a different ethnic, religious, and cultural background than those who had created the dykeland.

WHO WERE THE NEW ENGLAND PLANTERS?

Attracting settlers to Nova Scotia who would remain unquestionably loyal to their side had been a goal of British officials since 1713. The 1753 founding of Lunenburg, for instance, was carried out with "foreign Protestants," people of German and Swiss origins. It was not their ethnic background that mattered to British officials, but their Protestant religion; this was seen at the time as a key determinant of loyalty to a British monarch.

Where Did the Planters Settle?

Grand Pré was only one of many places the Planters settled in Nova Scotia. Other Planters came to Cornwallis, Falmouth, and Newport in what are now Kings and Hants counties. In central Nova Scotia they established Onslow and Truro, and along the South Shore they settled at Chester, New Dublin, Liverpool, Barrington, and Yarmouth. Still others went to Annapolis Royal and nearby Granville, and to Cumberland and Sackville (now New Brunswick) in the Chignecto area. In addition, Planters established Portland Point and Maugerville in what would later become New Brunswick.

Altogether, about eight thousand New England Planters came to settle in the region. Sometimes they settled where Acadians had been before, and in other instances they chose locations previously known only to the Mi'kmaq. In the span of roughly six years, 1755 to 1760, the combined effect of the Acadian Deportation and the coming of the New England Planters transformed Nova Scotia from a majority francophone to a majority anglophone colony.

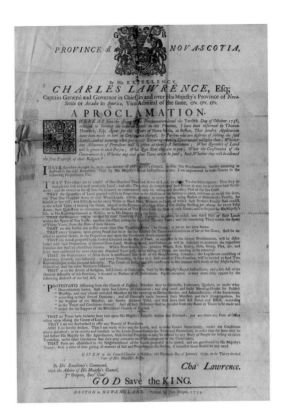

Hoping to attract settlers from New England, Governor Charles Lawrence of Nova Scotia issued this proclamation on January 11, 1759. The document states that one hundred acres of the province's woodland and fifty acres of developed land were available for every "White or Black Man, Woman, or Child."

Once the Acadians were removed from their lands at Grand Pré and elsewhere beginning in 1755, the British administration sought to attract New Englanders to Nova Scotia. Proclamations were issued in late 1758 and early 1759 to attract land-hungry settlers. Unable to move into western Massachusetts because of ongoing warfare, several thousand British colonists in Connecticut, Massachusetts, and Rhode Island decided to accept the relocation offered by the Government of Nova Scotia. These settlers are known collectively as the New England Planters.

SETTLEMENT AND USE

As noted previously, when the Planters arrived in the Grand Pré area they renamed it Horton Township. The name was to honour Lord Halifax, president of the Board of Trade in London, whose country house was called Horton Hall. The Planters took over whatever Acadian buildings were still standing and erected others of their own; some of the latter came prefabricated from New England.

To parcel out the land at Grand Pré, officials introduced a system of categorization: the most fertile land was the dykeland; then there were first- and second-division lots on the upland, as well as saltmarsh lots and woodland. According to oral tradition, the settlers' names were placed in one barrel and the lot numbers in another. Two separate draws determined who got what land. The end result was that people's lots were scattered far and wide. Many Planters later traded properties among themselves for more efficient holdings.

As the Acadians had done, the Planters chose to live along the uplands. They, too, established themselves in a diffuse manner, erecting new houses, barns, mills, and other buildings on the same ground rising from today's Hortonville, through Grand Pré toward Wolfville. Then again, to build on the dykeland was not an option: portions were flooded with seawater because of the

The Name Retained

Though New England Planters generally dropped the region's French place names, they called the vast dykeland the Grand Pré Marsh. Technically, to a French speaker, the name is redundant: *pré* means marsh, so the name translates as "great marsh marsh." But so it became, and so it remains today.

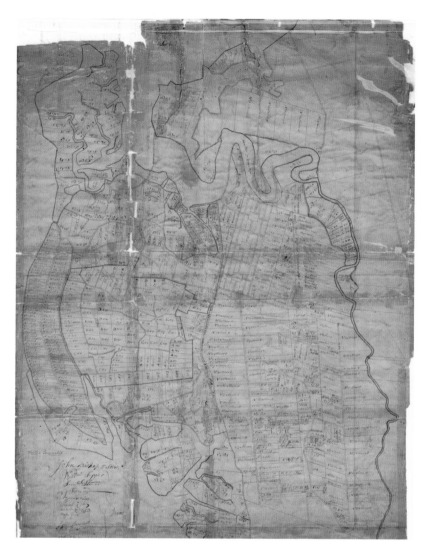

This plan shows how the lots were allocated to the Planters after they arrived at Grand Pré. The lots, distributed by a lottery, were on both the marshland (those not under water because of the breached dykes) and the uplands.

1759 storm. And it would have been foolish to build on the sections that were still dry and productive. The Planters had known before they arrived that the dykeland was the most fertile land at Grand Pré.

The cartographic and documentary evidence from 1760 onwards provides a clear indication of where the Planters settled and, by implication, insight into the Acadian community that predated them. Plans by Charles Morris and John Bishop, drawn in the 1760s and 1770s respectively, suggest strongly that some lots conceded to the Planters—we refer to the long, narrow lots on the south side of the dykeland—date from the Acadian period. These properties quite conceivably and plausibly date back to the former seigneurial concession of Alexandre Le Borgne de Belle-Isle. A number of boundary divisions still in place today are found on these old maps. While slightly wider today, so too are some of the roads in the present Grand Pré and Hortonville areas shown on the Morris and Bishop plans. What had been Acadian roads before 1755 became Planter roads five years later.

While there was definite continuity between the Acadian and Planter occupations of the uplands and dykeland of Grand Pré, there was one major difference: the Planters introduced a tight, rectilinear grid pattern, typical of eighteenth-century British and Anglo-American settlements (Halifax and Lunenburg come immediately to mind), in one area. The appeal of such tightly packed settlements was not only aesthetic; these settlements were also seen as more easily defensible in the event of an enemy attack. Recall that when the Planters came to Grand Pré, the Seven Years' War (1756–63) was still going on: the settlers and the administration in Halifax feared the French and/or Mi'kmaq might launch attacks.

An early map by Charles Morris contains the germ of the idea for a town grid on Grand Pré's upland. That 1748 map identified where Protestant settlers might be introduced into the area. Twelve years later, Morris's concept became reality. As things turned out,

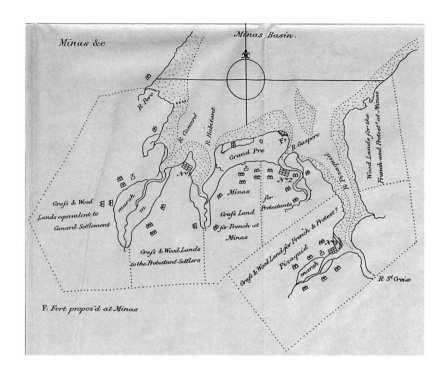

This 1748 map by surveyor Charles Morris illustrates one idea the British had to improve their relationship with Acadians. The two grid-like blocks on the map, marked No. 1 and No. 2, are where the British authorities wanted to establish Protestant settlers in the midst of the Acadian residents of the Grand Pré area. The plan was not implemented. Yet beginning in 1760, when New England Planters arrived, the British administration would introduce a town-grid block more or less where No. 2 is on the map.

however, there would be no attacks by the French or Mi'kmaq on Horton Township. So the Planters chose not to erect all their buildings according to the grid. Some preferred to live in a dispersed landholding pattern, much like their Acadian predecessors had done. Though the Horton grid was not fully used in the same manner as those at Halifax and Lunenburg, about 70 per cent of the 1760 rectilinear plan still exists today, in the form of several

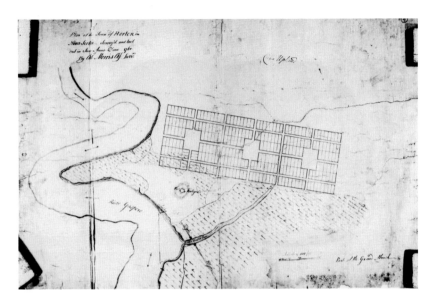

A detail of the Horton town grid, from a much larger plan drawn by surveyor Charles Morris in 1760.

unpaved and/or farm roads. The grid's survival across the two and a half centuries is remarkable. Then again, what has proven even more durable is the dispersed settlement pattern preferred by the active farming community, first the Acadians and then the Planters.

The biggest challenge faced by the Planters as they settled at Grand Pré was what to do with the flooded portions of the vast dykeland. These portions could not be given out or farmed. Since the Planters were unfamiliar with dyking practices and the construction of aboiteaux, it was an enormous challenge to them, as was how to reclaim—once again enclose and desalinate—the areas damaged or still covered by seawater. The Planters followed the most logical course; they turned for advice—and then assistance and labour—from the experts: the Acadians imprisoned in nearby Fort Edward, in what was now the Planter town of Windsor (formerly Pisiquid).

A group of men from the Grand Pré community carry out dyke maintenance. Though taken in the twentieth century, with the exception of clothing style, this photo presents a scene that remained constant along the dykes of Grand Pré and elsewhere since the late seventeenth and early eighteenth centuries.

One can only imagine how stunned the Acadians were to be asked—or more likely told—to do this. Whether willingly or reluctantly we do not know, but the Acadians did what was requested. They passed on to the newcomers the secrets of wetland transformation they and their ancestors had acquired. With that guidance, the Planters reclaimed the areas of the Grand Pré dykeland that had been flooded in 1759.

In yet another element of continuity with the Acadian period, the Planters retained and followed a similar pattern of local ownership and control over the dykeland. The same basic approach continues in the twenty-first century. Today, the individual farmers of the Grand Pré Marsh Body hold and work many of the same plots the Acadians and Planters farmed. Even more surprising perhaps, about 30 per cent of the fields on the dykeland retain precisely their pre-1755 size and shape.

Thanks to the transmission of knowledge and techniques from the imprisoned Acadians, the Planters who settled in Horton Township eventually became master dyke builders. They would maintain what the Acadians had built and enclosed, and eventually their descendants would add new dykes. Some projects were constructed on top what the Acadians had built; others were undertaken in areas the Acadians had not previously tackled. Most notably, the Planter descendants succeeded in raising the Wickwire Dyke in the early 1800s, reclaiming a large area on the western side of the great marsh.

THE DYKING LEGACY CONTINUES

John Young ("Agricola"), the foremost expert on agriculture in Nova Scotia in the early nineteenth century, offered an assessment of the Grand Pré marshland. Writing in 1822, sixty-two years after the Planters arrived, he wrote:

The construction in 1808 of the Wickwire Dyke on the west side of the Grand Pré Marsh (toward Wolfville) was a massive project undertaken by the descendants of the initial group of Planters. When completed, it opened up an additional 3,237 hectares for cultivation. Though later reduced in size by erosion from the Cornwallis River, it was nonetheless a great achievement.

The coast of the Bay of Fundy is unquestionably the garden of Acadia, and accordingly we find that the French planted themselves there on the first occupation of the country. They threw across those dikes and aboiteaux by which to shut out the ocean, that they might possess themselves of the rich marshes of Cornwallis and Horton, which prior to our seizure they had cropped for a century without the aid of manuring.... Spots in the Grand Prairies of Horton have been under wheat and grass alternately for more than a century past, and have not been replenished during that long period with any sort of manure.

The debt owed to the original builders of the dykes was not forgotten as time went by. Writing in the early 1880s, American horticulturist D. L. Boardman observed:

Grand Pré Dike is one of the oldest in Kings County and one of the best in the province. The old French had dikes here on the first occupation of the country, and there are now to be seen all over the Grand Pré remains of old dikes within those now doing their duty in

This 1820s view, entitled *Cape Blow-Me-Down, and the Bason of Mines*, depicts how the Minas Basin area flourished agriculturally in the half century following the arrival of the New England Planters.

keeping back the tide. These have been plowed down and leveled off in places, but it is not a difficult matter to trace them.

A generation later, the American biologist and writer Margaret W. Morley (1858–1923) was equally impressed by what the Acadians had first achieved and the Planters maintained. In 1905 she wrote, in much the same vein: "we cannot gaze upon the broad meadows before the door of Grand Pré without remembering the hands that first held back the sea."

Despite the political and military turmoil, especially the profound rupture of the Deportation, the landscape the Acadians cultivated at Grand Pré—dykeland and upland—has witnessed great continuity through to today.

THE PLANTERS IN
NOVA SCOTIA HISTORY

Though the consequences were dramatically different, the Planters, like the Acadians before them, would also wrestle with questions of their loyalty to the British administration. When their friends and relatives back in New England broke with Great Britain during the American Revolution (1776–83), the Planters in Nova Scotia did not follow suit. Although they had, only a decade and a half before, lived among those whose revolutionary sentiment would surge, those Planters who had come to Nova Scotia preferred neutrality. In so doing, they echoed the majority Acadian stance of twenty years before. As an outlet for their conflicted emotions, many Planters in Nova Scotia took part, in the mid-1770s, in a province-wide religious revival, the Great Awakening, led by evangelical preacher Henry Alline. According to the epigraph on his tombstone, Alline was "a burning and shining light and justly acclaimed the apostle of Nova Scotia."

Wherever the Planters settled in the 1760s, they exerted in the following decades considerable influence on Nova Scotia's culture,

The Great Awakening

The "Great Awakening" was initially a term used to describe the movement of evangelical enthusiasm and religious piety that swept through New England in the 1730s and 1740s. Much the same phenomenon, known as the second Great Awakening, developed in mid-1770s Nova Scotia, with Henry Alline (1748–84) as its charismatic leader.

Born in Newport, Rhode Island, Alline moved with his family to Falmouth, Nova Scotia, in 1760. At age twenty-eight he experienced a profound religious "rebirth," writing, "my whole soul seemed to be melted down with love." Prompted to become an itinerant preacher, he travelled from town to town spreading his "New Light" message. Many responded to his call and to that of other preachers, such as John Payzant and William Black, who also travelled across the Maritimes.

Historians point out that the difficult economic conditions at the time, compounded with the identity crisis the Planters were experiencing (because their former friends and relatives in the United States were breaking with Great Britain) made them particularly receptive to a movement emphasizing personal salvation.

landscape, and architecture. They are credited with showing particularly strong leadership in democratic government and educational reform. Some of the best-known buildings in today's Grand Pré are associated with the Planters: Crane house (1767), Calkin house (1768), Stewart house (1779), and Covenanters' Church (constructed between 1804 and 1811) are all much admired. In nearby Wolfville, Acadia University, though it dates from a few generations after their arrival in the province, has a link to the Planters. Former Canadian prime minister Sir Robert Borden (1854–1937) was a Planter descendant; moreover, he was born and raised in the village of Grand Pré. Recently, the 250th anniversary of the coming of the New England Planters to Nova Scotia was marked by numerous commemorative events across the province. Ceremonies drew descendants back to areas where their forebears

Old Church, Grand Pre, N.S.

Interior of the Old Church, Grand Pre, N.S.

One of the guarantees made by Governor Lawrence in 1759–60 to entice the Planters to immigrate to Nova Scotia was that they would be free to worship as they chose. As a consequence, settlers followed different faiths, not just the official Church of England. The Covenanters' Church reflects a New England meeting house style. Built at Grand Pré between 1804 and 1811, with the tower, belfry, and steeple added in 1818, it is the oldest standing Presbyterian church in Canada and a national historic site.

Planter Legacies

The New Englanders who came to Nova Scotia were mostly from Massachusetts and Connecticut, so it is no surprise that in their new settings they chose to erect houses, churches, and other buildings that resembled those they had known in their former towns and rural areas: a transplanted New England architectural style, one could say. Some Planter newcomers arrived with lumber, hardware, and other building materials to help them start their lives anew.

In addition to a distinctive building style, the New England Planters brought their religious faiths: most were Baptists or belonged to Congregational churches. This set them apart from the Church of England establishment in Nova Scotia. The Planters successfully pushed for a greater separation of church and state and for an end to the religious privileges Anglicans enjoyed.

had settled, and the events rekindled pride in what the original Planters accomplished.

Though the Planters put down deep roots in Horton and reshaped the area, a little more than a century later the community decided to reinstate the name the Acadians had used, Grand Pré. The change appears to be connected with the construction of the rail line in the 1860s, which carried large numbers of tourists to the "Land of Evangeline" during the summer months. These tourists expected to arrive in Grand Pré. By the 1870s, sure enough, this was the official name that greeted them at the train station and post office. Other name changes included an 1897 Act of Parliament, which saw Horton Landing become Hortonville. An earlier request to change the name of that area to Acacia (or Acadia) had been rejected.

It is understandable that there was a desire (and pressure) to go back to the original Acadian name or at least allude to that era. By the late nineteenth century, the name "Grand Pré" was recognizable across North America and in many parts of the world. How that happened and what it meant for the area is the focus of the next chapter.

CHAPTER 7

MEMORY AND RECOGNITION

Grand Pré Park is considered the most important Historic Site by the Acadian people. [It] must remain for future generations the example of a courageous people whose culture and actions shall enrich more and more the Canadian nation.

–Agreement between the Government of Canada and the Société Nationale l'Assomption, 1956

Beginning in the 1760s, a portion of the Acadian population, principally made up of those who had fled or gone into hiding as well as those imprisoned in various British forts, began to return to what today are the Maritime provinces. Only a minority of those who had been transported great distances ever returned. In most cases—Pubnico, Isle Madame, Menoudie, Malpèque, Memramcook, and Petcoudiac were the notable exceptions—New England Planters had occupied the former lands of the Acadians, meaning the Acadians could not return. Instead, the Acadians settled in many locations new to them across the Maritimes.

In the late nineteenth century, Acadian descendants participated in what is known as the Acadian Renaissance. Beginning in the 1860s and gaining momentum in the 1880s and 1890s, a spirit of perseverance and nationalism surged among Acadians throughout the Maritime provinces. The cultural elite that emerged in that movement organized a series

(Previous page) In 2008, as an inspirational event during the twenty-ninth Finale des Jeux de l'Acadie, an Atlantic-region-wide competition of young Acadians, all participants, dressed in their respective regional team colours, made the trip from Halifax to Grand Pré and posed for this photo.

Nelson Surette's evocative painting *The Return* presents a family coming back to the Maritimes a number of years after being forcibly removed during the Grand Dérangement. In rare instances, Acadians returned to their former land. Much more often, and definitely at Grand Pré, their valuable cultivated land had been taken by newcomers. Most returning Acadians had to begin their new lives somewhere else and learn new skills.

of national conventions, which in turn produced a flag, a national day, an anthem, and other markers of identity and pride. As the leadership surveyed its collective past, a few events and places stood out as having been especially formative and iconic. Grand Pré, and what it stood for, was high up on that list. Early in the twentieth century, a number of Acadian individuals and organizations began to commemorate their ancestors' bygone presence there and the forcible removal that had taken place.

Two major forces were at work to put such a focus on Grand Pré. One related to the many historical, literary, and artistic works that linked Grand Pré—more than any other Acadian village of the

The Acadian Renaissance

During the 1880s Maritime Acadians began to hold "national conventions" around the region to achieve political and cultural objectives. The first was at Memramcook, New Brunswick; the second was at Miscouche, Prince Edward Island. Quite quickly, the Acadian leadership chose a National Feast Day (August 15), a patron saint (Notre-Dame-de-l'Assomption), a flag, an anthem, and a motto.

In a related action, the Collège Saint-Joseph, a French-language Acadian classical college, was established in Memramcook in 1864, with university status. Almost overnight the college became a key institution involved in promoting the overall goal of preserving the language and culture of Acadians. Meanwhile in Nova Scotia, the Collège Saint-Louis and Collège Sainte-Anne were founded in 1877 and 1890.

As for Grand Pré and its symbolic importance, in 1895 Henri Léander d'Entremont published an article in the newspaper *L'Évangéline*, arguing that Acadians should honour their ancestors at the emerging tourist site at Grand Pré. A little over a decade later, concrete steps were taken in that direction.

The Société Nationale l'Assomption was the predecessor of today's Société Nationale de l'Acadie (SNA). The original Société played a leading role in the Acadian Renaissance by organizing many Acadian national conventions, including one at Grand Pré. Note that the name of the Bouctouche, New Brunswick, branch on the ribbon (left) is Évangéline.

pre-1755 era—to the Acadian Deportation. The other force was the Maritimes-wide Acadian Renaissance, which was seeking to find and generate pride and inspiration in the Acadians' past. Together, these two forces combined to transform a portion of the Grand Pré upland—initially a fourteen-acre area immediately adjacent to the enclosed dykeland—to make it an important historic site and tourist attraction in North America. Visitors of Acadian descent, whether they were living in the Maritimes, Quebec, Louisiana, France, or elsewhere, were coming to regard Grand Pré as the most cherished of all Acadian historical sites.

A TOURIST SITE

The best-known and most influential of the many literary and historical works connected to Grand Pré is unquestionably Henry Wadsworth Longfellow's *Evangeline, A Tale of Acadie*, published in 1847. The bucolic opening section of the epic poem is set in Grand Pré—an idealized Grand Pré, to be sure, yet nonetheless a wonderfully imagined, literary Grand Pré.

The story Longfellow told in his poem was of a young Acadian woman from Grand Pré called Evangeline, who is separated from her betrothed, Gabriel, during the Deportation. After they are exiled to separate southern British colonies, Evangeline spends the rest of her life travelling throughout what would become the

An Evangeline figure in the early twentieth century, along what looks to be a section of the Old Post Road.

The Worldwide Success of *Evangeline*

In the one hundred years following the first appearance of Longfellow's *Evangeline*, in 1847, it went through at least 270 editions and 130 translations. Though the *Evangeline* phenomenon began among non-Acadians—Americans first, then the British—Acadians, who came to know it through Pamphile Lemay's French translation, quickly embraced it. Lemay's adaptation differed significantly from the original poem by Longfellow, yet the central characters, the opening setting in Grand Pré, and the narrative arc all remained unchanged.

The first foreign-language adaptations were in German and Polish in 1851, followed by French and Danish in 1853, Swedish in 1854, Dutch and Italian in 1856, and so on around the globe. Illustrated editions began to appear in 1850.

Over the next century and a half, many artists offered their visual (often fanciful) interpretations of Grand Pré and other locales. When motion pictures came along, the story of Evangeline and the Acadian Deportation turned up in cinematic versions. Short, one-reel adaptations of the tale by Longfellow were produced in 1908 and in 1911. In 1913 the first feature-length film ever produced in Canada was a five-reel production of *Evangeline*. American film versions followed in 1919 and 1929.

Longfellow's book-length poem remains in print today, in many different editions.

United States in search of her beloved. She finally finds him on his deathbed in Philadelphia when they are both very old. While the specifics of the tale are fictitious, the gist of the epic poem is based on a story Longfellow had himself heard, of a young Acadian couple separated at the time of the Deportation.

Longfellow was not the first to write about the forcible removal of the Acadians in literary form, but his characters and plot line became by far the best known. The reason why the American poet selected Grand Pré as the setting for the opening of *Evangeline* came down to what he had learned about the Deportation. Longfellow never visited any part of Nova Scotia in person, but he had read Thomas Chandler Haliburton's *An Historical and Statistical Account of Nova-Scotia* (1829). In that book, Haliburton, using John Winslow's eyewitness account, describes what occurred at Grand Pré in 1755. Thus it was that Grand Pré, a real place with a tragic history, became the

For many years no level of government placed a commemorative marker at Grand Pré. The first government to do so was the Province of Nova Scotia, which in 1955 added a bust of the American poet Henry Wadsworth Longfellow to the park-like grounds that had evolved under the care of the Dominion Atlantic Railway (DAR).

opening location for a fictitious work. For the next century and beyond, Longfellow's poem, with its central figures, Evangeline and Gabriel, was by far the best-known interpretation of the Acadian

The Commercialization of Evangeline

Throughout the 1920s and 1930s the DAR, the Nova Scotia Information Service, and many private companies undertook promotions using images and slogans that made reference to Grand Pré and/or Evangeline. Depictions of the literary heroine showed up on a range of products, from soft drinks to car dealerships to chocolates.

This 1895 brochure, published a half century after the release of Longfellow's poem, speaks volumes about how important Evangeline had become to the tourism industry of Nova Scotia.

Deportation. Building on that extremely broad base, the Nova Scotia tourism industry would market Grand Pré and much of the Annapolis Valley as the "Land of Evangeline."

In 1869, at its newly opened Grand Pré railway station, the Windsor and Annapolis Railway Company (W&AR) hung a sign that read, *Welcome to the Land of Evangeline and Gabriel.* The next year saw the first organized railway tour of the "Land of Evangeline," by Americans from Boston. Acadians were not involved in these tourism developments, but a generation later they would take steps to reclaim Grand Pré in their own symbolic fashion.

AN HISTORICAL SITE

While it was Longfellow's epic poem that initially generated a public awareness of the ties between the Acadians and Grand Pré,

The old willow trees of "Evangeline's home," from the late 1800s.

it took the work of many others to transform the real Grand Pré into a location that could physically reflect the attachment people felt to the landscape and to what had happened there in 1755.

In 1907 the Wolfville jeweller and amateur poet John Frederic Herbin purchased land at Grand Pré containing ruins that were said to date back to the Acadian era. Herbin's mother was Acadian, and he felt a strong attachment to the place and what it represented. The oral tradition contends that the land Herbin bought contained vestiges of the old Acadian parish church, Saint-Charles-des-Mines, in which Acadian males ten and older were imprisoned in September 1755. Not far away was a well people claimed also dated back to the Acadian period. A little further on was the old Acadian burial ground. Then there were the silent witnesses to the events of 1755, the old willow trees. (The trees are highly visible in old photos of the area and many are still standing today.)

In 1908 the Government of Nova Scotia passed an Act to incorporate the trustees of the "Grand-Pré Historic Grounds." This

One of several concept drawings developed by landscape architect Percy Nobbs in 1919. What he envisioned would mostly come to pass.

was the first attempt by any government to safeguard the site at Grand Pré. It would be another half century before the federal government would get involved at Grand Pré. The absence of any direct governmental administration of the site meant there was a long period during which passionate individuals, concerned corporate interests, and the widespread Acadian community would shape the commemorative monuments and storylines at Grand Pré.

Herbin and the other trustees of the site sold the property, with its prominent ruins and old willows, to the Dominion Atlantic Railway (DAR) in 1917. Importantly, Herbin insisted that the church site be deeded to the Acadian people so they might erect a memorial to their ancestors. The DAR assumed responsibility for the Grand Pré site and engaged renowned architect Percy Nobbs to develop a detailed landscape plan for the grounds, complete with pathways, flower beds, and potential monument locations.

With Nobbs's drawings in hand, the rail company developed a park for those tourists looking to visit the location Longfellow had made famous in his epic poem. The brand new setting—a cross between a *jardin des plantes* and a commemorative cemetery—encouraged visitors to reflect on the Acadian tragedy of 1755. The first major artistic element added was a bronze statue of Evangeline, unveiled in 1920. The statue was produced by the celebrated Quebec sculptor Henri Hébert, of Acadian origin, and was a variation of an earlier design by his father, sculptor Louis-Philippe Hébert.

LIEU DE MÉMOIRE

Despite the commercialism of *Evangeline*, Acadians, beginning in the 1920s, showed increased interest in and attachment to Grand Pré. It was considered an evocative site that marked the saddest period of their ancestors' history. In 1921 the Société Nationale l'Assomption (predecessor of today's Société Nationale de l'Acadie [SNA]) held a portion of its eighth national convention at Grand Pré. At a special ceremony, the SNA took official possession of the church site and launched a fundraising campaign to build a memorial church on what was widely thought to be the ruins of

This postcard shows a pilgrimage to Grand Pré in 1924 (the year the Deportation Cross was erected) by Quebec newspaper *Le Devoir*.

the original parish church. The following year, 1922, Acadian workers began to build the Memorial Church (*l'Église Souvenir*), designed by architect René A. Fréchet. Acadians and friends and supporters from across Canada and the United States donated to the cause. The construction of Memorial Church was just one more example of the wave of Acadian nationalism that had been on the ascendant since the 1880s.

The Acadian community's commemoration efforts at Grand Pré continued over the next several years. In 1923 funds were raised for a sculpture of the Acadian patron saint, Notre-Dame-de-l'Assomption, to be placed inside the Memorial Church. The next year a group of Acadians and non-Acadians erected a poignant symbol of the 1755 Deportation: the iron cross, referred to as the Deportation Cross, was situated along the DAR rail line, about two kilometres from the Grand Pré site, at a dry creek bed believed

A 1930 event at the cross John Frederic Herbin erected to mark the Acadian cemetery. The cross is now called the Herbin Cross to honour the memory of the man who started the movement to protect and commemorate the bygone Acadian presence at Grand Pré.

By the time this large group of *Cadjens* (Cajuns) arrived at Grand Pré in 1936, the site was well established as a place of pilgrimage for all people of Acadian descent.

to be the spot where the area's Acadians had embarked in small boats during the Deportation. Later research demonstrated that the actual embarkation spot was Horton Landing (Vieux Logis). The iron cross was relocated accordingly in 2005.

Because of the various initiatives of the 1920s, Grand Pré became an ever more important pilgrimage site for Acadians. (So it was for many non-Acadians as well.) That the Deportation had been a terrible human tragedy was a sentiment deeply felt. People came not just from the Maritime provinces but from across North America and further abroad. In 1924 and 1926, Quebec-based newspaper *Le Devoir* organized group tours to Grand Pré. In 1930 and 1936, large contingents of Acadian descendants from Louisiana made the trip, marking the first official contact between *Acadiens* and *Cadjens* (Cajuns)—Acadians of the North and of the South—since the eighteenth century. A few decades later, in August 1955, thousands of Acadians from across North America gathered at what was then known as Grand Pré Park (today's Grand-Pré National Historic Site of Canada) to mark the two hundredth anniversary of the Deportation.

By 1955 all the major elements of a distinctive Acadian *lieu de mémoire* had been in place at Grand Pré for three decades: the Memorial Church, statue of Evangeline, Deportation Cross, old willows, stone cross raised by Herbin, well, and flower beds. Only a bust of Longfellow, added in 1955, came as a government action; all other memorials were erected by concerned citizens and organized groups, primarily within Canada but also from the United States.

RECOGNITION FROM NEAR AND FAR

In May 1955 the Historic Sites and Monuments Board of Canada (HSMBC), the arm's-length advisory body that recommends

A massive Acadian Congress is held close to the Memorial Church, 1955.

Who Are Today's Acadians?

Today the Acadian identity continues to evolve. No longer is it tied to living in what used to be Acadie, or to being a farmer or fisher, or even to practicing the Roman Catholic faith (although the latter attachment was once dominant). Today's Acadie is, some have observed, an imaginary country, a nation without the usual state connections. Acadie is a country without borders, observed Boutros-Boutros Ghali while secretary-general of the United Nations. Today's Acadian identity is rooted in an attachment to family history, to remembering and marking the past, and to building a bright future. And regardless of whether today's Acadians—or Cajuns as they call themselves in Louisiana—live in the Maritimes, Quebec, the United States, France, or anywhere else, they all regard Grand Pré as a sacred place.

designations of national significance to the responsible federal minister, concluded that the "Grand Pré Memorial Park possesses historical features which would make it eminently suitable as a National Historic Park." Negotiations began, and on December 14, 1956, the Société Nationale l'Assomption (SNA) finalized the sale of the commemorative park at Grand Pré to the Government of Canada. Five years later, in 1961, Parks Canada officially opened Grand Pré National Historic Park. Since that transition, Parks Canada has worked collaboratively with representatives of the

Acadian community to maintain the original commemorative monuments. The aim of both parties is that the site—as it is now called, rather than a park—fulfill its obligations as a national historic site and at the same time continue to be the principal *lieu de mémoire* for Acadians everywhere.

In 1995 the Government of Canada designated an even larger national historic site stretching from Long Island to the Gaspereau River, called the Grand Pré Rural Historic District. That site acknowledges the interconnected importance of dykeland and upland as a cultural landscape from the 1680s to the present, including the significance of not only what the Acadians accomplished but also the achievements of the New England Planters and the farming community that has evolved in more recent times. The breadth and nature of the "Rural Historic District" designation prompted some to wonder if the greater Grand Pré area might not have what is required to become a UNESCO World Heritage Site. The idea slowly grew in the local Kings County community and in Acadian hearts and minds far and wide.

THE ROAD TO UNESCO RECOGNITION

The first UNESCO World Heritage Sites were selected in 1978. More are added every year. In Canada the process begins with the

Grand-Pré National Historic Site of Canada

According to the HSMBC, there are three main reasons why Grand Pré is of national significance:

1) It was a centre of Acadian activity from 1682 to 1755.
2) It commemorates the deportation of the Acadians, which occurred at Grand-Pré in 1755.
3) It commemorates the strong attachment that remains to this day among Acadians throughout the world to this area, the heart of their ancestral homeland and symbol of the ties which unite them.

For more than 250 years this has been Horton Landing. Before that, to the Acadians, it was Vieux Logis. This landing area along the Gaspereau River witnessed two events of national significance: the tragedy of the Acadian Deportation and the coming of the New England Planters.

preparation of what is called a Tentative List. The country's first list was compiled in 1980, and by the end of the twentieth century it was time to compose a fresh one. One hundred thirty locations from all provinces and territories were studied, then assessed as to

UNESCO Criteria

The two criteria Grand Pré was submitted under were:

v. to be an outstanding example of a traditional human settlement, land-use, or sea-use which is representative of a culture (or cultures), or human interaction with the environment especially when it has become vulnerable under the impact of irreversible change;

vi. to be directly or tangibly associated with events or living traditions, with ideas, or with beliefs, with artistic and literary works of outstanding universal significance. (The Committee considers that this criterion should preferably be used in conjunction with other criteria.)

To see the overall World Heritage Site list, and a great deal more, please go to whc.unesco.org/en/list.

The living landscape of Grand Pré is a magical place both day and night.

whether they might meet the demanding criteria of UNESCO. In 2004 Canada announced a new Tentative List. There were eleven sites, of which two were in Nova Scotia. The Joggins Fossil Cliffs were inscribed on the World Heritage List in 2008. Four years later, it was the Landscape of Grand Pré's turn.

The process of submitting any site to UNESCO as a candidate for a World Heritage designation is long. Within each nation potential sites go through a rigorous process of research, evaluation, and clarification of significance. It's a process that takes several years. Then there's the year and a half after a nomination is made in February of any given year during which time international experts review and assess the nominated place. The candidate site must be found to be an exceptional example of the category it represents. It has to possess "outstanding universal value" under one or more criteria. There are ten possible criteria against which any nominated site is assessed, six for cultural sites (i to vi) and four for natural ones (vii to x).

In the particular case of Grand Pré, an organization was formed called Nomination Grand Pré. Its members represented the many interested and affected communities, and it had the support of all levels of government. Working collaboratively, Nomination Grand Pré completed the many reports and studies required to put forward an area to UNESCO as a candidate World Heritage Site.

A FINAL WORD

There are two main ways in which a world heritage site differs from a national historic site. Firstly, unlike a national historic site, which is dedicated to preserving, commemorating, and communicating a person, place, or event of historical importance in a particular country, a world heritage site possesses qualities that speak to everyone on the planet. Secondly, the key qualities need to be ongoing, not only of past consequence. So it is with the Landscape of Grand Pré World Heritage Site. It is both an enduring cultural landscape and an outstanding example of a distinctive approach to turning wetland into farmland and, through its evocative memorials and inspirational landscape, a place with a tragic history that has been transformed, for all humanity, into a symbol of reconciliation.

The official summary from UNESCO reads:

The Landscape of Grand Pré is an outstanding example and enduring model of the human capacity to overcome extraordinary natural challenges and cultural ordeals. It is a living agricultural landscape, claimed from the sea in the 17th century and still in use today applying the same technology and the same community-based management. It is also a powerful symbolic landscape for the Acadians who lived in harmony with the native Mi'kmaq people, were dispersed by the Grand Derangement, and symbolically re-appropriated it in a spirit of peace and cultural sharing with the English-speaking community.

Grand Pré: only two words, yet what an exceptional place.

ACKNOWLEDGEMENTS

The authors want to acknowledge how much they have benefited from the advice and suggestions of numerous people.

The following were members of the Working Group on the Outstanding Universal Value, back when Grand Pré was a candidate UNESCO World Heritage Site: Samuel Arseneault, Naomi Blanchard, Sherman Bleakney, Neil Boucher, Gérald Boudreau, Margaret Conrad, Graham Daborn, Jonathan Fowler, Stephen Henderson, Marc Lavoie, Barbara LeBlanc, Phyllis LeBlanc, Debra McNabb, Daniel Paul, Henri-Dominique Paratte, John Reid, and John Shaw.

Others who assisted in the evolution of this book were Roy Bishop, Sherman Bleakney, the Blomidon Naturalists Society, Theresa Bunbury, Catherine Cottreau-Robins, Fred and Betty Currie, Paul Delaney, Rebecca Dunham, Mark Eastman, Chrystal Fuller, Gordon Fulton, Gerald Gloade, Gordon Haliburton, Grand Pré Historical Society, Eileen Harris, Beth Keech, Kings Community Economic Development Agency, Kings Hants Heritage Connection, Guy LeBlanc, Jean Léger, Maurice Léger, Lucie Lebouthillier, Roger Lewis, Barry Moody, Jean Palmeter, Marilyn Perkins, John Pinkerton, Muriel K. Roy, Trudy Sable, Gary Shutlak, Lillian Stewart, Bria Stokesbury, Jan Sykora, Pat Townsend, Anjali Vohra, and Stephen White.

Claude DeGrâce and Christophe Rivet, who wrote the introduction, deserve extra special thanks. Without their assistance and support, this book would not likely exist at all.

BIBLIOGRAPHY

The authors are able to highlight only a small portion of what is readily available in English, in history and literature.

WEBSITES

Landscape of Grand Pré World Heritage Site: landscapeofgrandpre.ca

Parks Canada: pc.gc.ca/eng/lhn-nhs/ns/grandpre/index.aspx

BOOKS

Ancelet, Barry Jean, Jay Edwards, and Glen Pitre. *Cajun Country*. Jackson: University Press of Mississippi, 1991.

Arsenault, Georges. *The Island Acadians: 1720–1980*. Translated by Sally Ross. Charlottetown: Ragweed Press, 1989.

Aucoin, Réjean, and Jean-Claude Tremblay. *The Magic Rug of Grand-Pré*. Halifax: Nimbus Publishing, 1989.

Bleakney, Sherman. *Sods, Soil, and Spades: The Acadians at Grand Pré and Their Dykeland Legacy*. Montréal: McGill-Queen's University Press, 2004.

Brasseaux, Carl A. *The Founding of New Acadia: The Beginnings of Acadian Life in Louisiana*. Baton Rouge: Louisiana State University Press, 1987.

Brebner, John Bartlett. *New England's Outpost: Acadia Before the Conquest of Canada*. New York: Columbia University Press, 1927.

Brown, Wayde. "Percy Nobbs and the Memorial Garden at Grand Pré." *Journal of the Society for the Study of Architecture in Canada*, 32, 2 (2007) 29–38.

Butzer, Karl W. "French Wetland Agriculture in Atlantic Canada and Its European Roots: Different Avenues to Historical Diffusion." *Annals of the Association of American Geographers*, 92, 3 (2002) 452–70.

Clark, Andrew Hill. *Acadia: The Geography of Early Nova Scotia to 1760*. Madison: University of Wisconsin Press, 1968.

Conrad, Margaret, ed. *They Planted Well: New England Planters in Maritime Canada*. Fredericton: Acadiensis Press, 1988.

Conrad, Margaret, and Barry Moody, eds. *Planter Links: Community and Culture in Colonial Nova Scotia*. Fredericton: Acadiensis Press, 2001.

Daigle, Jean, ed. *The Acadians of the Maritimes: Thematic Studies*. Moncton: Centre d'études acadiennes, 1982.

Daigle, Jean, and Robert LeBlanc. "Acadian Deportation and Return." Plate 30 in *Historical Atlas of Canada. Vol. 1: From the Beginning to 1800*. Edited by R. Cole Harris. Toronto: University of Toronto Press, 1987.

Dawson, Joan. *The Mapmaker's Eye, Nova Scotia Through Early Maps*. Halifax: Nimbus Publishing and the Nova Scotia Museum, 1988.

Dunn, Brenda. *A History of Port Royal / Annapolis Royal, 1605–1800*. Halifax: Co-published by Nimbus and the Historical Association of Annapolis Royal, 2004.

Faragher, John Mack. *A Great and Noble Scheme: The Tragic Story of the Expulsion of the French Acadians from Their American Homeland*. New York: W. W. Norton, 2005.

Fowler, Jonathan, and Earle Lockerby. *Jeremiah Bancroft at Fort Beauséjour & Grand-Pré*. Kentville, NS: Gaspereau Press, 2013.

Griffiths, Naomi. *From Migrant to Acadian: A North American Border People, 1604–1755*. Montréal: McGill-Queen's University Press, 2004.

Gwyn, Julian. *Planter Nova Scotia, 1760–1815* (4 vols). Wolfville, NS: Kings–Hants Heritage Connection, 2010.

Haliburton, Gordon MacKay. *Horton Point: A History of Avonport*. Kentville, NS: Gaspereau Press, 1998.

Hatvany, Matthew. *Marshlands: Four Centuries of Environmental Changes on the Shores of the St. Lawrence.* Sainte-Foy, PQ: Presses de l'Université Laval, 2003.

Hodson, Chris. *The Acadian Diaspora: An Eighteenth-Century History*. New York: Oxford University Press, 2012.

Jobb, Dean. *The Acadians: A People's Story of Exile and Triumph*. Mississauga, ON: John Wyley & Sons Canada Ltd., 2005.

Johnston, A. J. B., and W. P. Kerr. *Grand-Pré: Heart of Acadie*. Halifax: Nimbus, 2004.

LeBlanc, Barbara, *Postcards from Acadie: Grand-Pré, Evangeline & the Acadian Identity*. Kentville, NS: Gaspereau Press, 2003.

Longfellow, Henry Wadsworth. *Evangeline, A Tale of Acadie*. Boston: William D. Ticknor & Company, 1847.

MacMechan, Archibald [McKellar]. *Red Snow on Grand Pré*. Toronto: McClelland & Stewart, 1931.

Marsters, Roger. "'The Battle of Grand Pré': The Historic Sites and Monuments Board of Canada and the Commemoration of Acadian History." *Acadiensis*, XXXVI, 1 (Autumn 2006) 29–50.

Moody, Barry. *The Acadians.* Toronto: Grolier, 1981.

Norton, Judith Ann. *New England Planters in the Maritime Provinces of Canada 1759–1800: Bibliography of Primary Sources.* Toronto: University of Toronto Press in association with Planter Studies Centre, Acadia University, 1993.

Perrin, Warren A., Mary Broussard Perrin, and Phil Comeau, eds. *Acadie Then and Now: A People's History.* Opelousas, LA: Andrepont Publishing, 2014.

Plank, Geoffrey. *An Unsettled Conquest: The British Campaign Against the Peoples of Acadia.* Philadelphia: University of Pennsylvania Press, 2000.

Reid, John G. *Six Crucial Decades: Times of Change in the History of the Maritimes.* Halifax: Nimbus, 1987.

Ross, Sally, and Alphonse Deveau. *The Acadians of Nova Scotia Past and Present.* Halifax: Nimbus, 1992.

Rudin, Ronald. *Remembering and Forgetting in Acadie: A Historian's Journey through Public Memory.* Toronto: University of Toronto Press, 2009.

Silver, Alfred. *Three Hills Home.* Halifax: Nimbus, 2001.

Stevens, Maynard G. *Where They Rest in Peace: A Guided Tour of Seven Historic Cemeteries in Kings County, Nova Scotia.* Kentville, NS: Gaspereau Press, 2001.

Taylor, M. Brook. "The Poetry and Prose of History: *Evangeline* and the Historians of Nova Scotia." *Journal of Canadian Studies*, 23 (1988) 46–65.

IMAGE CREDITS

All images courtesy of Parks Canada, except where noted below.
Parks Canada photographers/designers: Chris Reardon (pp. 7, 11, 102 [top]);
Christophe Rivet (9, 10, 12, 19, 21, 47, 66, 112); Steven Slipp (18, 68); Tim Daly (41)

iv: Courtesy Mark Eastman

2: Courtesy Canada Post

4, 85, 88: Reproduced with permission of the NS Department of Natural Resources

5, 94: Courtesy Dan Soucoup

13: iStock

14: Courtesy Rob Fensome, Atlantic Geoscience Society. Modified by Andrew MacRae
  from original compiled by John Wade for *The Last Billion Years* (2001)

17: Courtesy John Shaw, Geological Survey of Canada

22, 25, 36, 83, 87, 90, 102 (bottom), 103: Nova Scotia Archives

27, 39: Courtesy Rebecca Dunham

28: Leonard Paul

29: Courtesy Confederacy of Mainland Mi'kmaq

32, 113: Courtesy Roy Bishop

34, 60: Library Archives Canada

35, 43, 52: Nova Scotia Museum

40: Courtesy Fort Anne National Historic Site

45: Courtesy Le Village historique acadien de la Nouvelle-Écosse

53: Courtesy Sherman Bleakney

54: Courtesy Jonathan Fowler

57: Courtesy Victor Tétrault

62, 78, 98: Courtesy Municipality of Clare permanent collection

75, 99: Musée Acadien, Université de Moncton

p. 77: Courtesy George Rodrigue Foundation

89, 100: A. L. Hardy

p. 91: Courtesy Dalhousie University Library, Special Collections

p. 96: Courtesy Gerald Mallet

p. 105: Université de Moncton (Fonds Placide Gaudet, 1.20.17)

110: Courtesy François Gaudet

INDEX

Numbers set in italics refer to images

A

Acadian Congress *109*
Acadian Deportation (Grand Dérangement) 7, 8, 11, 61, 67–8, 71, *74,* *75,* 79, 82, 92, 98–102, 107–08, 111–12, 114
Acadian Renaissance 97, 99
Acadia University 2, 93
"Agricola." *See* Young, John
Alline, Henry 92–93
American Revolution 92
Annapolis Basin 19–20, 40
Annapolis Gut 30
Annapolis Royal 33, 38, *39,* 61–4, 66. *See also* Port-Royal
Argall, Sir Samuel 37
Avon River (rivière de l'Ascension; rivière Pigiguit) 44

B

Back, Francis *31*
Barrington 82
Battle of Grand Pré (1747) 10, 64, *65, 66*
Bay of Fundy 14–5, 17, 20, 30, 81, 91
Beaubassin 42, 59, 63–64, 68
Beaubassin ridge 70
Bedford Basin 16
Belle Isle *43*
Belle-Isle, Alexandre Le Borgne de 86
Bishop, John 86
Black, William 93
Bleakney, Sherman *53*
Boardman, D. L. 91
Board of Trade (London, England) 84
Borden, Sir Robert Laird 11, 93
Boston, MA 103
Bouctouche, NB 99
Bousfield, Ed 20
Budrot (Starrs) Point 75, 77

C

Cajuns 77, *108,* 110. *See also* Louisiana, KY
Canada Post 2
Canada (Quebec) 64. *See also* Quebec
Canard River (rivière aux Canards) 43–4, 76
Canso (Canseau) 36, 61
Cape Blomidon 17, 30
Cape Breton Island (Île Royale) 42, 60, 65, 68
Cape Split 30
Champlain, Samuel de 37
Charlesfort 38–39. *See also* Fort Anne
Chester 82
Chezzetcook 68
Chignecto 64, 66, 69, 71–2, 82
Chignecto Isthmus 38, 41, 61, 69
Church, Benjamin 59
Church of England 94–5
Cobequid/Cobeguit. *See* Truro
Collège Sainte-Anne. *See* Université Sainte-Anne
Collège Saint-Joseph 99
Collège Saint-Louis 99
Confederacy of Mainland Mi'kmaq 28, *29*
Connecticut 76, 83, 95
Cornwallis 82
Cornwallis River (rivière des Habitants; rivière Saint-Antoine) 43–4, 52, 76, 90
Covenanters' Church 11, 93, *94*
Craig, George *75*
Cumberland, NB 82

D

d'Anville, Duc 64
d'Entremont, Henri Léander 99
d'Entremont, Philippe Mius *45*
Deportation. *See* Acadian Deportation
Deportation Cross 11, *57,* 79, *106,* 107, 109

Dominion Atlantic Railway (DAR) 102, 105, 107
Duvivier, François Du Pont 63

E

Evangeline, A Tale of Acadie 9, 100–02, 106. *See also* Longfellow, Henry Wadsworth
Evangeline Statue 7, 11, *72*, 109

F

Falmouth 82, 93
Father Pacifique 30
Finale des Jeux de l'Acadie *97*
Fort Anne 27, 37, 39
Fort Beauséjour 65–66, 69, *70*, 72
Fort Cumberland 69, 71, 73
Fort Edward 66, 73
Fort Gaspareaux (Gaspereau) 66, 69
Fort Lawrence 69–70
Fort Monckton. *See* Fort Gaspereaux
Fort Sainte Marie de Grâce 39
France 37, 39, 41, 46, 60–61, 63–64, 69, 77, 79, 100, 110
Francis, Bernie 24
Fréchet, René A. 107

G

Gaspé peninsula, QC 23, 26, 29
Gaspereau 74
Gaspereau Lake 26
Gaspereau River (rivière "des Gasparots") 10, 26, 44, 52, *57*, 76, 81, 111, *112*
Geological Survey of Canada 17
Georges Island 79
Ghali, Boutros-Boutros 110
Gloade, Gerald 28
Government of Canada 110–11
Government of Nova Scotia 84, 104
Grand Dérangement. *See* Acadian Deportation
Grand Pré Marsh 6, 8–9, 11, 26, 33, *47*, *54*, 55, 84, 90
Grand Pré Marsh Body 55, 89
Grand Pré Park 97, 108

Grand Pré Road 66
Great Awakening 92–93.
Great Britain 60–3, 69, 92–3

H

Habitant Creek (rivière des Vieux Habitants) 44
Habitants River 76
Haliburton, Thomas Chandler 102
Halifax 36, 41, 57, 62, 66, 68–9, 71, 79, 86–7, 97
Halifax, Lord 84
Hébert, Henri 106
Hébert, Louis-Philippe 106
Herbin Cross 11, *72*, *107*, 109
Herbin, John Frederic 1, 13, *72*, 104–05, 107
Historic Sites and Monuments Board of Canada (HSMBC) 66, 109, 111
Hood, Elder Stephen 30
Horton *88*, 91, 95
Horton Landing (Vieux Logis) 11, 24, 26, 42, *57*, 73–75, 95, 108, *112*
Horton Township (Grand Pré) 11, 84, 87, 89
Hortonville 6, 11, 55, 84, 86, 95

I

Isle Madame 97

J

Jefferys, C. W. *65*, *80*
Joggins Fossil Cliffs 113

K

Kingsport 26
Kluskap (Glooscap) 26, *28*, *29*, 30

L

La Have (La Hève) 38
Landry, Cécile 43
Landry, Claude 43

Landscape of Grand Pré Society 2–3
Launay-Razilly, Claude de 39–40
Lawrence, Governor Charles 69, 71, 83, 94
LeClercq, Christian 29
Le Devoir 106, 108
l'Église Souvenir. *See* Memorial Church
Lemay, Pamphile 101
Lescarbot, Marc 37
L'Évangéline (newspaper) 99
Lewis, Roger 24
Liverpool 82
London, England 71
Longfellow, Henry Wadsworth 1, 5, 7,
    9, 100–01, *102*, 103, 109. *See also*
    Evangeline, A Tale of Acadie
Long Island *iv*, 10, *21*, 32, 111
Lords of Trade 71
Louisbourg 56, 63–66
Louisiana, KY 77, 100. *See also* Cajuns
Lunenburg, (Mirligouèche) 66, 68, 82, 86–7

M

Malpèque, PEI 97
Maryland 76
Massachusetts 69, 71, 76, 83–4, 95
Maugerville, NB 82
Melanson, Charles 44
Melanson, Pierre 42–4
Melanson Settlement (Saint-Charles) 26, 44
Membertou, Chief 34, 37
Memorial Church (l'Église Souvenir) 7,
    11, 53, 106–07, *109*
Memramcook, NB 42, 97, 99
Menou d'Aulnay de Charnisay, Sieur
    Charles de 39–40
Menoudie 97
Menou, Joseph de 40
Minas (Les Mines) 33, 42, 44, 57
Minas Basin *iv*, 8, *12*, *13*, 14–16, *17*, 18,
    20, 26, 30, 32, 38, 42, 44, 52, 57,
    72–3, *76*, 81, 91
Mirligouèche. *See* Lunenburg
Miscouche, PEI 99
Missaguash River 70
Mius d'Entremont, Marie-Marguerite 42–4
Mius d'Entremont, Philippe 44
Monckton, Lt.-Col. Robert 69
Monts, Sieur de 37

Morley, Margaret W. 92
Morris, Officer Charles 59, 69–70, 78, 86
    1748 map of Horton Township *87*
    1760 map of Horton Township *88*
Murray, Capt. Alexander 73
Musquodoboit 24

N

New Dublin 82
Newport 82
Newport, RI 93
Nobbs, Percy *105*
Noble, Col. Arthur 64, 66
Nomination Grand Pré 113–14
North Grand Pré 6, 10
Northumberland Strait 16, 19
Notre-Dame-de-l'Assomption 99, 107
Nova Scotia Council 69–70
Nova Scotia Department of Agriculture 9
Nova Scotia Museum 24, 43

O

Old Post Road 5, 66, *100*
Onslow 82

P

Pacifique, Father (Henri Buisso de
    Valigny) 30
Parker, Lewis *48*
Parks Canada 1, 10, 40
Parrsboro 17
Paul, Leonard *28*
Payzant, John 93
Pennsylvania 76, 101
Petitcodiac (Petcoudiac) 42, 97
Philipps, Governor Richard 62
Picard, Claude *56*, *74*
Pisiquid. *See* Windsor
Portland Point, NB 82
Port-Royal 36–39, 41, 44, 46, 63
    habitation 34, 37
Port Royal (Scots) 37–9
Prince Edward Island (Île Saint-Jean)
    16, 19, 42, 60, 65
Pubnico 45, 97
Pugwash 24

Q

Quebec 28, 100, 106, 110. *See also* Canada (Quebec)

R

Rand, Silas 30
Razilly, Isaac de 38
Rhode Island 84
Riverside-Albert, NB (Shepody/Chipoudie) 42
rivière aux Canards. *See* Canard River
rivière de l'Ascension. *See* Avon River
rivière "des Gasparots." *See* Gaspereau River
rivière des Habitants. *See* Cornwallis River
rivière des Vieux Habitants. *See* Habitant Creek
rivière Pigiguit. *See* Avon River
rivière Saint-Antoine. *See* Cornwallis River
rivière Sainte-Croix. *See* St. Croix River
Rodrigue, George 77

S

Sable, Trudy 28–9
Sackville, NB 82
Saint-Charles. *See* Melanson Settlement
Saint-Charles-des-Mines 56, 72, 78, 104
Saint-Étienne de La Tour, Governor Charles de 44
Saint John River 24, 65
Saint Mary's University 28
Seven Years' War (1756–63) 86
Shaw, John 17
Shepody/Chipoudie. *See* Riverside-Albert, NB
Shirley, Governor William 69
Smith, Douglas 24
Smith-Francis orthography 24
Société Nationale de l'Acadie. *See* Société Nationale l'Assomption
Société Nationale l'Assomption (SNA) 97, 99, 106, 110
St. Croix River (rivière Sainte-Croix) 43
Surette, Nelson *62, 78, 98*

T

Terriot, Pierre 43
Thibodeau, Catherine 43
Tooke, Susan *37, 58, 76*
Treaty of Aix-la-Chapelle 65
Treaty of Utrecht (1713) *60*, 61
Truro (Cobequid/Cobeguit) 42, 68, 82

U

UNESCO 1, 3, 6, 10, 18, 55, 111–14
United States 101, 107, 110
Universite de Sainte-Anne 2, 99

V

Valigny, Henri Buisson de. *See* Father Pacifique
Vienneau, Azor *43, 52*
Vieux Logis (Horton Landing) 42, 57, 66
Village Historique Acadien de la N-É 45
Villiers, Nicolas-Antoine Coulon de 64
Virginia 37, 77

W

Wallace-Ferguson, Birgitta 40
War of the Austrian Succession 65
War of the League of Augsburg 59
War of the Spanish Succession 60
White, Stephen 61
Wicken, William 61
Wickwire Dyke *90*
Windsor (Pisiquid) 66, 68, 71, 73, 76, 88
Windsor and Annapolis Railway Company (W&AR) 103
Winslow, Lt.-Col. John 71–74, 77, 79, 102
Wolastoqiyik (Maliseet) 24
Wolfville 6, 7, 26, 43, 55, 84, 93

Y

Yarmouth 19, 82
Young, John ("Agricola") 81, 90

STORIES OF
OUR PAST

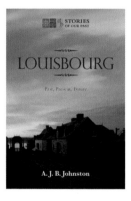

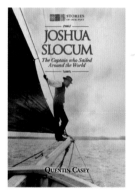